CONTEMPORARY'S

AMAZING CENTURY

BOOK THREE
1945 TO 1960

D0620028

**Developed by Contemporary Books, Inc., and General
Learning Corporation, Northbrook, Illinois**

Copyright © 1992 by Contemporary Books, Inc.
All rights reserved

No part of this publication may be reproduced, stored in a
retrieval system, or transmitted in any form or by any means,
without the prior written permission of the publisher.

Published by Contemporary Books, Inc.
Two Prudential Plaza, Chicago, Illinois 60601-6790
(312) 540-4500
Manufactured in the United States of America
International Standard Book Number: 0-8092-4017-3

Published simultaneously in Canada by Beaverbooks, Ltd.
195 Allstate Parkway, Valleywood Business Park
Markham, Ontario L3R 4T8 Canada

Library of Congress Cataloging-in-Publication Data

Amazing century.
     p.   cm.
    Includes indexes.
    Contents: bk. 1. 1900–1929 — bk. 2. 1929–1945 — bk. 3.
1945–1960
    ISBN 0-8092-4020-3 (pbk. : v. 1). — ISBN 0-8092-4018-1
(pbk. : v. 2). — ISBN 0-8092-4017-3 (pbk. : v. 3)
    1. United States—Civilization—20th century.
2. Civilization, Modern—20th century.   I. Contemporary
Books, inc.
E169.1.A47186   1992
973.9—dc20
                                        91-35292
                                        CIP

Editorial Director
Caren Van Slyke

Assistant Editorial Director
Mark Boone

Project Editor
Sarah Conroy

Editorial
Christine M. Benton
Pat Fiene

Editorial Production Manager
Norma Fioretti

Production Editor
Jean Farley Brown

Cover Design
Georgene Sainati

Cover Photo
© Michael Hart, FPG
International

Executive Editor
Laura Ruekberg

Managing Editor
Alan Lenhoff

Associate Editor
Miriam Greenblatt

Art Director
Ami Koenig

Research
David Bristow
Sam Johnson
Terese Noto
Therese Shinners
Betty Tsamis
Deborah Weise

To Our Readers

*The arrival of television . . . the nightmare of cold
war and the Korean war . . . the talent of sports
stars Jackie Robinson and Althea Gibson . . . the
rock 'n' roll revolution . . . the glamour and
excitement of 1950s Hollywood . . .*

In the pages of this book are some of the biggest
news stories of their day. The photographs and
stories in this book reach out to us. They tell
about people and events that have helped to
shape this century – and make our nation what
it is today.

Though you may not know all the faces and
places, you'll recognize many of the stories
behind them. You'll see that today's news
stories have their roots in the past – and that we
have many things in common with the people
who came before us. We learn from their
tragedies and benefit from their triumphs.

In pictures and in words, each of the books in
the *Amazing Century* series highlights a different
time period in this century. See for yourself.
Thumb through the pages of this and all the
Amazing Century books, and discover the way
we were.

The Editors

Arts and Entertainment

Sports

SWEET, SMOOTH AND SASSY—the beautiful Bel Air Sport Coupe. You can see and feel the solid quality of its Body by Fisher.

...lled with grace and great new things

CHEVROLET

1 USA

It looks agile, graceful and easy to handle — and it more than lives up to its looks! Chevy offers fuel injection and America's first and only triple-turbine transmission.

You expect something pretty special in the way of driving pleasure the very first time you take charge of a new Chevrolet. Those clean, graceful contours hold a promise of quicksilver responsiveness. And there's something about the...

car lives up to all its "advance notice"—and then some! Horsepower ranging up to 245* translates your toe-touch into cream-smooth motion. You find that turning a corner is almost as easy as making a wish. And you see how Chevrolet's solid sureness of control makes for safer, happier driving on city streets, superhighways and everything in between.

If you drive a new Chevrolet with Turbo-glide (an extra...

Money Matters

Crime, Punishment, and the Law

Science and Technology

T I M E · L I N E

1947
Jackie Robinson
becomes first
black player
in major-league
baseball

Marshall Plan
sends U.S. aid
to help rebuild
postwar Europe

1950
Senator
Joe McCarthy
starts 4-year
nationwide
"red scare"
by accusing
government workers
of being
Communists

North Korea
invades
South Korea,
triggering
Korean War

1945
World War II
ends

United Nations
is established

1952
U.S. grants
Puerto Rico
commonwealth
status

U.S. explodes
first hydrogen
bomb

1949
National Basketball
Association
is founded

33d–34th U.S. Presidents

Harry Truman

1945	1946	1947	1948	1949	1950	1951	1952

1957

Crisis in
Little Rock,
Arkansas,
as federal troops
must guard
Central High School
to ensure
peaceful
racial integration

Space Age begins
with launch
of Soviet
satellite *Sputnik I*

1954

*Brown v.
Board of Education
of Topeka*
rules that
racial segregation
in public schools
is unconstitutional

1959

Alaska and Hawaii
become 49th
and 50th states

Fidel Castro
takes control
of Cuba

1955

Bus boycott
in Montgomery,
Alabama, protests
segregation on
public buses

1953

Korean War
ends

1958

United States
launches
Explorer I

**Dwight
Eisenhower**

1953	1954	1955	1956	1957	1958	1959	1960

The World After the War

WORLD WAR II:
The Allies Close In

Source: U.S. Department of Defense

During the final years of the war, the Allies closed in on Germany from all directions.

In 1939, German dictator Adolf Hitler sent his armies into Poland. Great Britain and France came to Poland's aid – and World War II had begun. The war pitted Axis powers against Allied nations. By 1942, the Axis powers – Nazi Germany, Italy, and Japan – had overtaken France, Poland and most of Eastern Europe, and much of the South Pacific. The Allied nations – Great Britain, France, the United States, and (after 1941) the Soviet Union and China – fought to stop the Axis powers. Other nations joined in too. In all, 35 countries, with one-half of the world's population, took part in the war.

D-Day

At first, the war went badly for the Allies. Then the tide began to turn. The beginning of the Axis' fall was D-Day – June 6, 1944. On that day, Allied forces invaded the coast of France, which was controlled by Nazi Germany. Hundreds of bomber planes and planes loaded with troops took off from England. They flew across the English Channel, a waterway that separates England from France and the rest of Europe. Soon after midnight, the soldiers began parachuting down to earth. At the same time, almost 5,000 ships crossed the channel. They carried not only troops but also tanks, guns, ammunition, food, clothing, and medical supplies. The land attack on France's Normandy coast began at dawn. The entire operation was led by American general Dwight D. Eisenhower, whom most people called "Ike."

Within days of the Normandy landing, the Soviet Union attacked Nazi Europe from the east. Gradually, Allied armies squeezed Germany tighter and tighter. The war was turning the Allies' way.

The Yalta Conference

The winners, as the saying goes, get to write the history books. They also decide what to do with the losers. Even before the end of the war, Allied leaders were planning what to do with Germany. Twice in less than 30 years, Germany had triggered a world war. The Allies wanted to make certain that it would not do so again.

In February 1945, the leaders of the three major Allies—Great Britain, the United States, and the Soviet Union—met at Yalta, a Russian seaside resort. Prime Minister Winston Churchill spoke for Great Britain. President Franklin D. Roosevelt spoke for the United States. Premier Joseph Stalin spoke for the Soviet Union. Together, they were known as the "Big Three."

The Big Three decided to divide Germany into four zones of occupation. Each of their countries would control one zone. France, which borders Germany on the west, would occupy and control the fourth zone. When the Allies were sure that Nazi influences were gone, they would reunite the four zones into a single nation.

The Big Three also decided to divide the German capital of Berlin into four zones. But there was a problem: the city lay deep within the Soviet zone of Germany. The only way Great Britain, France, and the United States could get to their parts of Berlin was through the Soviet zone—but there was tension between these Western allies and the Soviets.

A Military Bargain

The future of Germany was not the only item the Big Three discussed at Yalta. They also talked about Eastern Europe.

By 1945, Soviet troops had occupied the Eastern European countries of Bulgaria, Czechoslovakia, Hungary, Poland, and Romania. The Soviets had freed these countries from the Nazis. Stalin thought that if these nations were friendly to the Soviet Union after

the war, they could help protect his country against another German invasion.

For their part, Churchill and Roosevelt wanted Soviet help in defeating Japan. Japan was still a strong enemy in February 1945. British and American military leaders were afraid that invading Japan might cost more than a million lives. If the Soviet Union joined the struggle against Japan, fewer British and American lives would be lost.

So Churchill and Roosevelt made a deal with Stalin. Stalin agreed to declare war against Japan after Germany surrendered. In exchange, he was given control over Eastern Europe. However, Churchill and Roosevelt made Stalin promise that he would hold free elections in the countries of Eastern Europe.

The Big Three meeting in Yalta, February 1945. From left to right: Winston Churchill (Great Britain); Franklin Roosevelt (U.S.); Joseph Stalin (USSR).

After the war, the nations of Eastern Europe were under Soviet control. So were the Baltic states. Germany was divided into four zones of occupation.

In May 1945, Germany surrendered. Japan surrendered in August. About 15 million soldiers and 20 million civilians had died in World War II. And future peace was still not certain, for Stalin controlled Eastern Europe.

An Iron Curtain

Stalin never kept his promise of free elections. At a Big Three conference — held in Potsdam, Germany, in July and August 1945 — he explained why: "A freely elected government in any of these East European countries would be anti-Soviet, and that we cannot allow."

After World War II ended, Soviet troops remained in Eastern Europe. Between 1945 and 1948, all the nations of Eastern Europe became Communist. Like the Soviet Union, they were dictatorships. Only the Communist party was allowed to exist. The government controlled what was printed in newspapers and said on radio and TV. It told artists what to paint and authors what to write. Factories and stores were owned by the government instead of individuals. People were rarely allowed to travel,

OCCUPATION
of Germany and
Eastern Europe

Zones of German Occupation

- American
- British
- French
- Soviet

Under Soviet Control

- Annexed Areas
- Baltic States
- Communist Eastern Europe

Europe: Before and After World War II

As a result of World War II, several European nations changed their boundaries. Other nations lost their independence. For instance, the Baltic states — Estonia, Latvia, and Lithuania — had been independent before the war. By the end of the war, they had become part of the Soviet Union. The Soviet Union also gained eastern Poland, northern Romania, and bits of Finland and Czechoslovakia. The Soviet Union's boundaries were now the same as they had been before World War I. Poland lost land to the Soviet Union but gained land from Germany. These and other changes are shown on the maps.

even from one city to another. And the secret police arrested anyone who opposed the government.

In March of 1946, Winston Churchill made a speech at Fulton, Missouri. He described the situation in Europe this way: "A shadow has fallen upon the scenes so lately lighted by the Allied victory. . . . an iron curtain has descended across the Continent [of Europe]. Behind that line . . . [people] . . . are subject in one form or another . . . [to] control from Moscow." After Churchill's speech, people have used the term *iron curtain* to describe the invisible wall separating Communist from non-Communist countries.

Not all Communist countries in Eastern Europe liked their new governments. In the late 1950s and 1960s, East Germany, Poland, Hungary, and Czechoslovakia all tried to get out from under Soviet control. Hungary's anti-Communist movement was especially strong. For a while, its government declared that Hungary was a neutral country – not part of the Communist world. The Soviet Union, however, sent in troops and tanks to put pro-Communists back in power. There was bloody fighting between troops and citizens. Finally, the Communists regained control of Hungary. The Soviets also used military strength to keep Communists in charge of the other countries behind the iron curtain.

Two Germanys

In spite of the Yalta and Potsdam meetings, the Allies could not agree about Germany's future. Great Britain, the United States, and other Western countries believed that Germany might not go to war again if it had a strong economy. The Soviet Union, on the other hand, wanted a weak Germany.

In 1948, the Western powers made their move. Great Britain, France, and the United States announced a plan to combine their three zones into one German nation, the Federal Republic of Germany (West Germany). The Soviets were very upset. They had lost close to 20 million people in World War II. They were afraid of a strong Germany. So they made a move of their own. They blockaded the Western zones of Berlin. No trucks, railroads, or canal boats could bring in supplies from the West. Stalin hoped to force the Western powers either to agree to a weak, divided Germany or to leave Berlin.

But the Western powers stood firm. They refused to agree to a weak, divided Germany. They also refused to leave Berlin. Instead, they organized an airlift to supply the people of West Berlin. For more than a year, American, British, and French cargo planes kept busy. They flew in more than 2 million tons of food, coal, medicine, and other supplies. They even flew in candy for the children of Berlin. Finally, in May of 1949, Stalin gave up. He lifted the blockade.

Soon after, the Soviet zone of Germany became the German Democratic Republic (East Germany). West Berlin – although surrounded by East Germany on all sides – was considered part of West Germany. ■

When the Soviets blockaded West Berlin in 1948, the Western allies organized an airlift to keep the city supplied. Here, American workers build a new runway in West Berlin.

The West Reacts to Communism

The Soviet Union could control most of Eastern Europe because its soldiers were there. But what about other European nations? Was there anything to prevent Soviet influence from spreading further?

The Truman Doctrine

President Harry S. Truman – who became president when Roosevelt died in April 1945 – believed there was. He did not want to go to war against the Soviet Union. Instead, he wanted to help European nations strengthen their governments. He also wanted to help these countries strengthen their economies and become richer. That way, their people would have faith in their government. They would not vote for local Communist parties. Nor would they support Communist-led fighters trying to overthrow their governments. Truman called his policy *containment.*

The first test of containment came in 1947. Both Turkey and Greece were in danger of turning to communism. So Truman asked the U.S. Congress for money to help them. He put it this way:

"... every nation must choose between alternative ways of life. ...One way of life is based upon the will of the majority. ... The second way of life is based upon the will of a minority forcibly imposed upon the majority. ... I believe that it must be the policy of the United States to

President Truman asking Congress for $400 million to help Greece and Turkey. Truman wanted to keep those countries from becoming Communist.

support free peoples who are resisting attempted subjugation [conquest] by armed minorities or by outside pressures."

Congress agreed. The United States decided to send $400 million in military and economic aid to Turkey and Greece. The Turks and the Greeks strengthened their economies and their governments. They held off Communist-led fighters and did not turn to communism.

The Marshall Plan

On June 5, 1947, General George C. Marshall, the American secretary of state, made a speech at Harvard University. In the speech, he suggested that the United States send money,

food, and machinery to the nations of Europe – including those controlled by the Soviet Union. His plan, soon called the Marshall Plan, was designed to help democracy survive in Europe. Marshall said, "Our policy is directed not against any country or doctrine but against hunger, poverty, desperation, and chaos."

Europe needed plenty of help in 1947. From shore to shore, Europe had been torn apart by World War II. Factories, roads, and railroads were in ruins. People needed food, clothing, housing, and fuel. Unemployment was sky-high.

Between 1948 and 1952, the Marshall Plan poured more than $13 billion into 16 European nations.

An American officer (far right) watching as Greek soldiers prepare to fire at Communist rebels. With U.S. support, Greece held off the Communists.

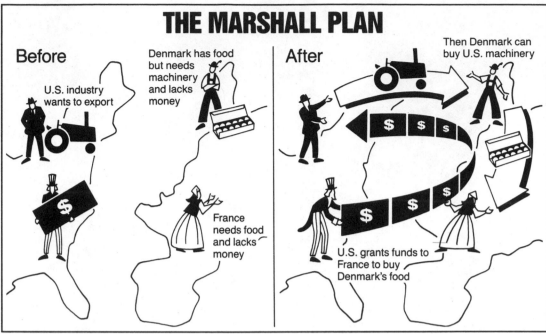

THE MARSHALL PLAN

Before

U.S. industry wants to export

Denmark has food but needs machinery and lacks money

France needs food and lacks money

After

Then Denmark can buy U.S. machinery

U.S. grants funds to France to buy Denmark's food

Source: Silver Burdett Ginn Inc.

As the drawing shows, the Marshall Plan was designed to help Europe recover from the war and to provide new markets for U.S. products.

As a result of the Marshall Plan, the nations of Western Europe were able to rebuild. They recovered from the war.

THEN & NOW

After World War II, Germany had been divided into two countries: East and West Germany. In 1961, Communist East Germany built the Berlin Wall to separate the two countries. For nearly 30 years, the wall divided East from West.

In November 1989, East Germany let its citizens cross through the wall to the West. Within a year, the wall was almost completely gone—much of it torn down by joyful citizens. And on October 3, 1990, the two Germanys "reunified," or became one country again. The new Federal Republic of Germany held its first national election in December 1990.

In fact, their farms and factories were soon turning out more goods than before the war.

The Soviet Union and the nations of Eastern Europe, however, did not recover from the war quickly. They turned down the U.S. offer of help. Stalin saw the Marshall Plan as just an attempt to spread capitalism—and he wanted nothing to do with it. ∎

"I believe that it must be the policy of the United States to support free peoples," said President Truman in 1947. *Do you agree? Should the United States get involved in foreign wars to protect other people's freedom?*

Should the United States get involved in civil wars—wars between groups of citizens in their own nations—if the United States believes one side is in favor of freedom and the other is not?

Some people say the United States should give less aid to other countries and spend the money here at home. Do you agree? Why or why not?

Trying Again: The United Nations

The League of Nations, formed after World War I, was supposed to settle arguments among nations peacefully. But the league could not prevent World War II. Why had it failed? One reason was that the United States had not joined the league. A generation and a war later, the United States had another chance. Would we again turn our back on world affairs? Or would we join other nations to help keep peace?

The answer came in 1945. On April 25, leaders from 50 nations—including the United States—met in San Francisco. After months of talks, they organized the United Nations.

The United Nations, or UN, stated these points in its charter:

1. We the peoples of the United Nations are determined to save the generations of people yet to come from the horrors of war.

2. We state again our faith in the basic human rights, in the dignity and worth of the human person, in the equal rights of men and women, and of nations large and small.

3. We will unite to preserve international peace and security. And we will try to bring about the economic and social advancement of all peoples.

The U.S. Senate had taken four months to decide *not* to join the League of Nations. This time, the Senate spent only six days in debate. The vote to join the UN was 89 to 2. ■

Some Americans think our country should get out of the United Nations—or at least stop paying for 25 percent of its expenses.

How do you feel about the UN? Do you think that an international group can help keep peace worldwide?

The United Nations logo (above) is recognized worldwide. The U.S. joins the UN in 1945 (below). The logos represent various UN agencies.

Declarations of Independence

After World War II, nations on the losing side lost power and territory. Oddly enough, nations on the winning side also began to lose territory. Their *colonies*—distant lands controlled by powerful countries—began to gain independence.

In some colonies, people had to fight for their freedom. The Indonesians, for instance, fought against their former Dutch rulers for four years. Indonesia became a free nation in 1949. The Algerians, who fought against their French rulers for seven years, became independent in 1962.

Sometimes, independence came peacefully. For example, the Philippines had been under U.S. control since 1898. In 1946, the United States kept its promise and freed the

The map shows how the United Nations divided India into two countries, India and Pakistan. East Pakistan is now the nation of Bangladesh.

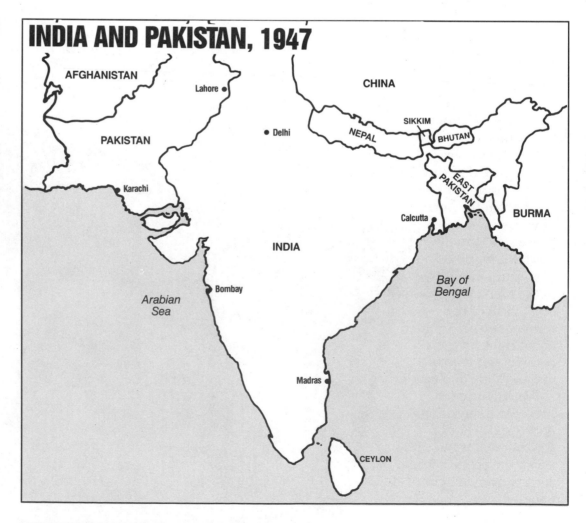

INDIA AND PAKISTAN, 1947

AFGHANISTAN

Lahore

PAKISTAN

Karachi

CHINA

NEPAL

SIKKIM

BHUTAN

Delhi

EAST PAKISTAN

Calcutta

BURMA

INDIA

Bombay

Arabian Sea

Bay of Bengal

Madras

CEYLON

Philippines. Across the globe, another great country – India – also gained its independence peacefully. India had been controlled by Great Britain since 1757. After years of nonviolent resistance, the Indians won their freedom from Britain in 1947.

Still, freedom for India came with bloodshed. Religious conflict caused the fighting. Most people of India followed one of two religions: Hinduism or Islam. For centuries, Hindus and Muslims (believers in Islam) had mistrusted and mistreated each other. When the British agreed to give India its independence, Hindu and Muslim leaders decided that each religious group should have its own nation. As a result, when the British left, the United Nations formed two countries: India, a mostly Hindu nation; and Pakistan, which was mostly Muslim. But many people were afraid to live in a country dominated by another religion. So Hindus flowed into India, and Muslims flowed into Pakistan. In all, about 12 million people changed homelands – and many thousands of them died in fighting along the way.

The State of Israel

It was the summer of 1947 when a ship called the *Exodus–1947* neared the shores of Palestine. Aboard were 4,500 Jewish refugees from Europe. They had survived the horrors of the Nazi death camps. Now, they were looking forward to entering the ancient Jewish homeland of Palestine.

But it was not to be. Instead, the *Exodus–1947* was stopped by British battleships. The British – who at that time ruled Palestine – put the Jews onto other ships and sent them back to Europe.

The action shocked the world. It also pointed to difficult questions: What should become of Palestine? What should become of the Jewish refugees?

Thousands of Muslims (left) journeying from India to Pakistan in 1947. Indian leaders Mahatma Gandhi (below right) and Jawaharlal Nehru (below left) talking in 1946. Gandhi led India's nonviolent struggle for independence. Nehru later became India's first prime minister.

Israeli leader David Ben-Gurion (above) reading Israel's Declaration of Independence on May 14, 1948. The map (right) shows how the UN divided Palestine.

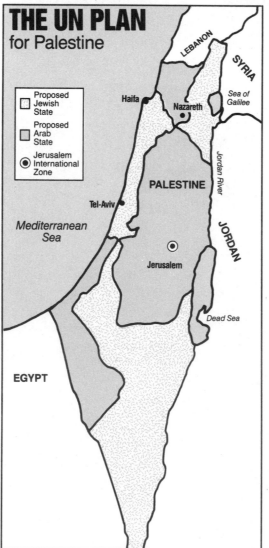

THE UN PLAN
for Palestine

- Proposed Jewish State
- Proposed Arab State
- ⊙ Jerusalem International Zone

LEBANON
SYRIA
Haifa
Nazareth
Sea of Galilee
Jordan River
PALESTINE
Tel-Aviv
Mediterranean Sea
JORDAN
⊙
Jerusalem
Dead Sea
EGYPT

Both Arabs and Jews lived in Palestine. Both groups claimed the land as their own. The Arabs argued that Palestine had been part of the Arab Empire 1,300 years before. Therefore, they said, it should be an Arab nation. The Jews argued that Jews had lived in Palestine for more than 3,000 years. Therefore, they said, it should be a Jewish state. Furthermore, in 1917 the British government had promised the Jewish people a national home in Palestine. Also, the Nazis had murdered 6 million European Jews in the Holocaust. The Jews felt they needed their own country—a place to go if another Hitler came along.

Great Britain finally turned the matter over to the United Nations. The UN decided that the Arabs and the Jews were both right. So it made a compromise. Palestine would be divided into three parts. One part would be an Arab state. Another part would be a Jewish state called Israel. The third part would be Jerusalem. This city—which is sacred to Jews, Christians, and Muslim Arabs—would be run by an international group.

On May 14, 1948, British troops pulled out of Palestine, and Israel was established. ∎

The Cold War— and a Hot Spot

The United States and the Soviet Union had been allies during World War II. But the two superpowers were very different. The United States, a democracy, practiced capitalism. The Soviet Union, a dictatorship, practiced communism. After the war ended, each nation feared the other's power and mistrusted the other's goals. They began the cold war. A cold war is a political battle. Rival countries do not actually shoot at each other, but they try to gain more power throughout the world. They try to spread their own political beliefs to other countries.

To gain more power, the Soviet Union set up Communist governments in Eastern Europe. The United States wanted friendly democracies in Western Europe, so it sent those countries economic and military aid. Both sides built up their supplies of atom bombs and other weapons. And each side threatened the other. "We will bury you," said Nikita Khrushchev, the new leader of the Soviet Union.

The Korean War Breaks Out

Because of the cold war, faraway Korea soon became a hot spot. Japan had taken over Korea in 1910. Near the end of World War II, Soviet and American troops swept the Japanese out. The Soviets occupied the northern part of Korea. The Americans occupied the south. The boundary between the two was the 38th parallel (see map).

By 1949, the Soviet and American troops had pulled out of Korea. They

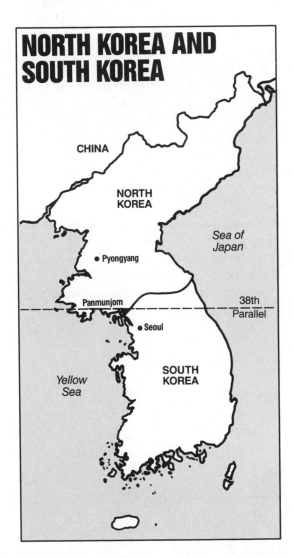

NORTH KOREA AND SOUTH KOREA

CHINA

NORTH KOREA

• Pyongyang

Sea of Japan

Panmunjom

38th Parallel

• Seoul

Yellow Sea

SOUTH KOREA

In 1950, the Communist North Korean army crossed the 38th parallel into South Korea. The war ended in 1953 near that line.

left behind them two separate nations: North Korea and South Korea. North Korea's leader was a Communist. South Korea's leader was not. But both men were dictators. And both claimed the right to rule all of Korea.

On June 25, 1950, troops from Communist North Korea crossed the 38th parallel into South Korea.

President Truman immediately decided to help the South Koreans resist the invasion. Two days later, the UN voted to do the same. Eventually, more than 20 nations sent troops or medical units to Korea to resist the Communists. The troops were commanded by the American general Douglas MacArthur.

A Fateful Decision

At first, it seemed as if the North Koreans were winning. They pushed UN soldiers back almost to the southern tip of Korea. Then, the United States began pouring in tanks, guns, and fresh troops. By the end of September, the North Koreans had been pushed back across the 38th parallel.

Now the UN had to make a decision. Should its troops stop? They had pushed the invaders back. Or should they invade North Korea?

At this point, a warning came from China. The Communists under Mao

Zedong had won the Chinese civil war in 1949. Communist China was friendly with Communist North Korea. The Chinese government warned that it would not allow its neighbor to be destroyed. Nor would it sit back and let the Americans come to the Chinese border. But the UN ignored the warning. It gave MacArthur the go-ahead to enter North Korea.

China Enters the War

By mid-October 1950, UN troops had swept across North Korea. They had almost reached the border of China. Then, on November 26, some 300,000 Chinese soldiers poured into North Korea. Once again, UN troops were pushed south of the 38th parallel.

So far, the UN policy had been to fight only a "limited war"—that is, a war only within Korea. Now, however, MacArthur began demanding that the United States carry the war to China. He had three goals: first, to blockade China's coast; second, to bomb Chinese factories and railroads; and third, to invade southern China.

President Truman refused. He felt that an all-out war with China would be "the wrong war at the wrong place, at the wrong time, and with the wrong enemy." He also feared that attacking Communist China would bring the Soviet Union into the war. That, in turn, would mean World War III.

MacArthur, however, went over the president's head. He took his message directly to the American public. For example, he sent a message calling for a new American foreign policy. He sent a letter attacking Truman's policies to the Republican leader in the U.S. House of Representatives. Finally, on April 11, 1951, Truman fired MacArthur. The president then appointed General Matthew B. Ridgway in his place. Under Ridgway, UN troops once again fought their way

General Douglas MacArthur (left) talking with President Truman (right) in October 1950. Later, when MacArthur demanded that the U.S. invade China, Truman fired him.

up to the 38th parallel. This time, they did not continue further north.

"I Shall Go to Korea"

In July of 1951, the two sides began peace talks. More than a year later, they were still talking.

In October of 1952, General Dwight D. Eisenhower – the Republican candidate for president – made a dramatic statement. If elected, he would go to Korea in person and end the war. Ike won the election in a

President-elect Dwight Eisenhower (left) eating lunch with U.S. troops in Korea. Ike had promised to go to Korea to try to end the war.

The "Old Soldier"

It was the largest crowd the city had ever seen. Thousands of Washingtonians cheered as the car carrying General MacArthur moved slowly through the streets. Many of the people were cheering his work in World War II, when he led Allied forces against Japan. Many were also showing how angry they were that President Truman had fired him as head of the UN troops in Korea.

The next day, MacArthur spoke to the U.S. Congress. His eyes filled with tears as he spoke about his years in the army. He ended his speech:

I still remember the refrain of one of the most popular . . . ballads [songs] of that day, which proclaimed, most proudly, that "Old soldiers never die. They just fade away." And like the old soldier of the ballad, I now close my military career and just fade away – an old soldier who tried to do his duty as God gave him the light to see that duty. Goodbye.

The next day, telegrams poured into the White House. Almost all of them criticized the president for his action.

But Truman held firm. He reminded his critics that under the U.S. Constitution, setting foreign policy is the job of the country's political leaders, not its generals. "I fired him because he wouldn't respect the authority of the President," Truman said years later. "He disobeyed orders, and I was Commander-in-Chief, and either I was or I wasn't. So I acted as Commander-in-Chief and called him home. . . . A civilian . . . has to run the armed forces. The men who wrote the Constitution understood that. . . ."

A few weeks after MacArthur's speech, the nation's top military leaders appeared before Congress to support Truman's action. Gradually, most American people changed their minds. Though they respected MacArthur, they decided that the president had done the right thing after all when he fired MacArthur.

Nikita Khrushchev addressing the United Nations in 1960. Just four years earlier, he had told the United States, "We will bury you."

landslide. He flew to Korea. But it was not until seven months later, in July 1953, that the two sides finally agreed to stop fighting.

Results of the War

Neither side really won the Korean War. On one hand, North Korea was prevented from taking over South Korea. The UN had "contained" communism. On the other hand, there were still two Koreas rather than one. Neither gained any territory from the other. In addition, more than 2 million people had been killed or wounded. Most of them were Korean civilians.

However, the Korean War had two important results. First, it stretched the cold war across the whole world. That is, it showed that tensions between the United States and the Soviet Union could break out *anywhere*. Second, for the first time, countries did not want to use their strongest weapon—nuclear bombs—for fear of starting a third world war. ■

U.S. vs. USSR

Many U.S. magazines helped build up American feelings against the Communist "Reds"—the Soviet Union. The articles listed below, for instance, appeared in *Reader's Digest* in 1950 and 1951.
- "Is War with Russia Inevitable?"
- "Where the Menace to Freedom Lies"
- "Europe's Old Nightmare Returns"
- "Can We Still Save America?"
- "Outlaw the Communist Party!"
- "We Can Win the Cold War—*in Russia*"
- "The Men the Reds Hate Most"
- "Why Russia Won't Attack This Year"
- "The War We Are Losing"
- "Are American Weapons Good Enough?"

Many Americans remember the cold war fears of the 1950s and early 1960s. Interview three or four who remember. Ask them how the cold war affected their lives. Ask them how they felt about the Soviet Union then and how they felt about the breakup of the union in 1991.

After President Truman had fired General MacArthur as commander in chief in the Korean War, the president said, "MacArthur . . . was in total defiance of my orders as President and as Commander-in-Chief . . . our Constitution [calls for] civilian control of the military." Do you agree that the president should control the military? Why or why not? How would you respond to someone who said, "But military officers know more about war"?

A Communist at Our Doorstep

Havana, Cuba. New Year's Day, 1959. Suddenly, black-and-red flags hung from buildings and automobiles throughout Cuba's capital. Along with the flags were portraits of a young man with a heavy black beard. He was Fidel Castro, whose followers had just overthrown Cuban dictator Fulgencio Batista. The black-and-red flag stood for "The Twenty-Sixth of July Movement." Castro had started his war against Batista on July 26, 1953.

At first, most Cubans were delighted with Castro's victory. He got rid of government officials who had stolen public funds. He promised that Cubans could vote for whomever they wanted. He took land from the rich and said he would divide it up among the poor.

But Castro did not keep most of his promises. Poor people were not given farms of their own. Instead, they were drafted to work on large government-owned farms. There were no free elections. Instead, many Cubans who were against Castro were jailed or shot. Thousands of people fled the country. The government took over the leading newspapers. It also took over mines, factories, sugar mills, banks, and hotels that were owned by Americans and other foreigners.

At first, the United States did not oppose Castro. It hoped he would solve Cuba's economic and social problems. Then, Castro began criticizing the United States. He appeared on television and talked about America's "sins." He accused the United States of trying to set up an empire in Central America. He said the United States was plotting against Cuba.

In 1960, Castro signed trade agreements with several Communist nations, including the Soviet Union and China. The following year, he announced what many people suspected: he himself was a Communist.

He was also just 90 miles away from the United States. ■

Fidel Castro (above center) fought for nearly six years before taking control of Cuba in 1959. Later, he announced that he was a Communist. The map (left) shows that Cuba is only 90 miles from Key West, Florida.

Booms: Buying, Building, and Babies

The war was over. It was as if the world could finally come up for air. And five years of war had been preceded by 10 years of economic hard times. Now, in 1946, Americans wanted a better life. During the war, Americans did not have all the food they wanted; now, they wanted big supermarkets. They had saved tin for the military; now, they wanted to drive steel monsters—big cars. Instead of making do, they made demands—for new cars, houses, electric appliances, and all the "modern conveniences."

Thanks to the new products and new wealth of postwar America, the 1950s saw an explosion of fads, including the Hula Hoop.

Buying Power

The U.S. economy was ready to produce what the people wanted. Industry boomed. Sales of automobiles doubled between 1947 and 1953. In

Fads of the Fifties

In the 1950s, a new material was suddenly everywhere: plastic. It was part of dozens of fads in the postwar decade—including Hula Hoops, tiny building blocks, unbreakable records, and unstoppable yo-yos.

Fads caught on with Americans of all ages. Youngsters used Silly Putty to transfer pictures from comic strips. They played with the coiled metal spring called Slinky—making it crawl downstairs. Upstairs, father brushed his teeth for the second time with whiskey-flavored toothpaste. Mother practiced for her cha-cha lesson on the plastic (there it is again!) dance-step mat.

The automobile was the biggest fad of all. Americans spent more time than ever in their cars. They went to drive-in restaurants and drive-in movie theaters.

Every era has its fads. But thanks to the new products and the new wealth of postwar America, the 1950s saw an explosion of them.

filled with grace and great new things

SWEET, SMOOTH AND SASSY—the beautiful Bel Air Sport Coupe. You can see and feel the wind quality of its Body by Fisher

CHEVROLET
USA

It looks agile, graceful and easy to handle—and it more than lives up to its looks! Chevy offers fuel injection and America's first and only triple-turbine transmission.

You expect something pretty special in the way of driving pleasure the very first time you take charge of a new Chevrolet. Those clean, graceful contours hold a promise of quicksilver responsiveness. And there's something about the low, action-poised profile that tells you Chevy's a honey to handle.

It doesn't take long to find out that this

car lives up to all its "advance notice"—and then some! Horsepower ranging up to 245* translates your toe-touch into cream-smooth motion. You find that turning a corner is almost as easy as making a wish. And you see how Chevrolet's solid sureness of control makes for safer, happier driving on city streets, superhighways and everything in between.

If you drive a new Chevrolet with Turbo-glide (an extra-cost option), you'll discover triple-turbine takeoff and a new flowing kind of going.

Come sample *all* these great new things!
SEE YOUR AUTHORIZED CHEVROLET DEALER

*270-h.p. high-performance engine also available at extra cost. Also Ramjet fuel injection engines with up to 283 h.p. in Corvette and passenger car models.

Americans bought record numbers of new cars in the 1950s. Among the most popular was the '57 Chevy Bel Air.

1953, Americans spent over $30 billion on leisure activities such as sports events, televisions, and phonograph records. Women's stockings came back in style. They had been scarce during the Great Depression and rationed during World War II. Now they were a big part of women's fashion.

Advertisers made buying seem patriotic. They appealed to the anti-Communist mood of the time. To buy, they said, was to show how the American system was better than Soviet communism.

The 1950s were also years when large corporations hired many people and made lots of money. Huge "chain" stores such as Sears and Walgreens began to force small family-owned stores out of business. Fast-food restaurants and motels became part of the American scene. And suddenly, the suburban shopping center was becoming busier than the city "downtown" business area.

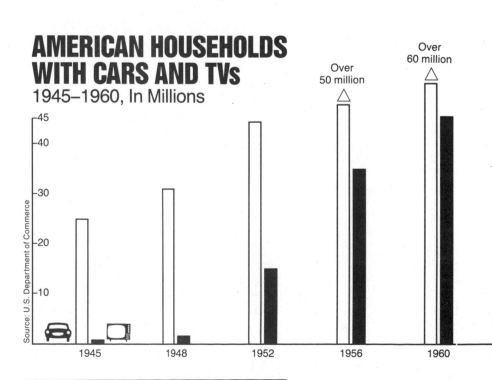

AMERICAN HOUSEHOLDS WITH CARS AND TVs
1945–1960, In Millions

Source: U.S. Department of Commerce

Over 50 million
Over 60 million

45
40
30
20
10

1945   1948   1952   1956   1960

Why were so many people so interested in moving to the suburbs? There was a variety of reasons.

For one thing, the American Dream of owning a family home was now within the reach of many people. The G.I. Bill of Rights helped World War II veterans get loans to pay for new homes. People wanted to escape noisy cities and crowded apartment buildings. They wanted their own yard, trees, and mailbox. These things became symbols of success.

In addition, it was becoming easier to live in the suburbs. Our great superhighway systems were built in the postwar years. Once, it had taken hours to reach communities outside the city. Now, thanks to the highways, it took less time. Meanwhile, loans from the Veterans Administration (VA) and the Federal Housing Administration (FHA) helped war veterans pay for the move to the suburbs.

Suburbs like Levittown, New York, boomed in the late 1940s and early 1950s. After World War II, many young veterans and their families moved to the suburbs.

Suburban Sprawl

In the 1950s, suburbs seemed to explode onto the American landscape. Small towns had always flanked large U.S. cities. But suddenly, these small towns—and many new ones around them—became the place to be.

Levittown: Instant Suburb

From a Long Island potato field, a new crop sprang up in the late 1940s. A huge suburb of cheap houses grew faster than potatoes—and at a greater profit.

The housing developers, Levitt and Sons, first offered their suburban dream to veterans who had housing loans from the federal government. But the houses soon became popular with hundreds of thousands of others.

Levittown's instant success was due to very low prices. The average American earned about $3,000 a year in 1950. So at $7,990, a home in Levittown was a bargain. Each had a fireplace, a built-in TV, a barbecue, a private yard, and a garage. These were luxuries many of Levittown's young army veterans and their families had never dreamed of.

William J. Levitt's picture appeared on the cover of *Time* magazine. People renamed other communities "Levittown." Then the nickname was jokingly replaced: so many babies were born all at once in Levittown that people called it "Fertility Valley."

Places like Levittown boomed in the early 1950s. However, people soon wanted houses that did *not* look like their neighbors' houses. For that reason, Levittown and similar suburbs became less popular by the late 1950s.

Moving to the suburbs was also a way for veterans and their families to express their confident new self-image. The G.I. Bill not only helped pay for new homes. It also helped pay for college educations. Suddenly, people who never had been able to go to college had the opportunity. They knew it could lead to higher-paying jobs. This changed the way veterans and their families thought of themselves. They saw themselves as having better chances and more choices. They took this new confidence with them to the suburbs.

There was also an unhappy reason for the flight to the suburbs. Many middle-class white citizens were alarmed to see blacks moving into their neighborhoods—even in small numbers. Fearing the blacks, they chose to move rather than get to know their new neighbors. For that reason, many inner-city neighborhoods became mostly black. Most suburbs in the 1950s were almost entirely white.

As strange as it may sound, even the fear of communism caused people to move to the suburbs. In 1951, the *Bulletin of Atomic Scientists* encouraged people to move away from the cities. Why? If the Russians attacked the United States with nuclear bombs, they would attack the cities. More people would survive if Americans were more spread out.

For the Children
But one reason for the move to the suburbs was more important than any other: children. People believed that their children would have better lives in the suburbs than in the city. The 1950s were a very child-centered time. Parents had lived through war and the Depression; they were determined that their children would not suffer as they had. And there were more children than ever. Families were getting larger in the 1950s. It was the middle of the so-called "Baby Boom"—the huge increase in the birthrate after World War II.

American life went through incredible changes between 1945 and 1960. Take the average World War II veteran. When Joe Smith returned from the war late in 1945, he moved into his parents' small apartment. He shopped at the corner store his parents had used for years. He wondered if his uncle could get him a factory job so he could earn enough money to marry Joan. By 1959, Joe, a college graduate, had a high-paying job. He and Joan lived in a suburb and shopped at the big shopping center in their town. They had four children, whose days were filled with school, ballet class, Cub Scouts, and Little League baseball. And Joe and Joan felt different; they were middle-class now. Sometimes Joe walked around his neatly mowed backyard in the evening. He thought, How far we have come! ■

Make a list of good things about city living. Then list some benefits of suburban living. Which lifestyle do you prefer? Write a few sentences to tell how you feel.

This house in Levittown was a bargain at just $7,990. It had a fireplace, a built-in TV, a barbecue, a private yard, and a garage.

Images of Women

"Back to the kitchen!" is what many voices of the postwar period seemed to say to women. During World War II, many women had worked outside the home; the men were off at war. After the war, however, women were expected to give up their jobs and return to the home to be wives and mothers. Women were *allowed* to work. But women who wanted more than motherhood were thought to be strange.

Everything in American culture seemed to push women back into the home. Women's magazines printed stories with such titles as "Have Babies While You're Young" and "Cooking Is Fun to Me!" TV shows like "Father Knows Best" and "Make Room for Daddy" featured stay-at-home mothers. TV commercials were filled with women who worried about getting their kitchen floors waxed and their children's clothes as clean as possible. Movies sent the same message. Stars like Doris Day played women who could be happy only if they got married. Every message girls and women got seemed to be pushing them in the same direction.

At the same time, women who did work outside the home got little encouragement. They usually could get only low-status jobs. Their pay was very low. Women were paid no more than 60 cents for every dollar a man earned, even when they did the same work. The idea of women doctors, lawyers, or engineers seemed un-American to many people. After all, women did these jobs in the Soviet Union—proof that it was wrong.

At times, the grudge against working women was out in the open. Popular magazines such as *Ladies Home Journal* wrote that women should *want* to stay home. Some even said that unmarried women over 30 should not be allowed to be teachers. Why not? Because obviously there was something wrong with them that could hurt the children! It was not an easy time for a woman to be single or to work outside the home.

And yet . . . something interesting was happening. The move to the suburbs had an important, but unspoken, result: it separated people from older members of their family. Young men and women did not take their parents and grandparents with them to the suburbs. The older people usually stayed in the city. For young women, this meant more work. They raised their children and kept house without the help of mothers, grandmothers, and other female relatives. They had little help and had to take more responsibility. It made them stronger and more independent.

It also made them wonder, Is this all there is? From their suburban "paradise," they looked out at the world their TV sets showed them. To many, it was a wide, exciting world, a world of opportunity. Yes, women in commercials worried about floor wax. But there was also "TV college" on educational stations—and many women "went back to school" this way.

Sometimes things can start to change so quietly that we don't see it happening. This quiet change was taking place in middle-class women in the 1950s. A decade later, the emotions that were quietly building would explode. ∎

Being a woman in the 1950s was very different from being a woman today. Interview someone who was a young housewife then. Ask her what she thought of her life then. Did she enjoy it? How does she feel she has changed since then?

Most women stayed at home during the 1950s. This busy housewife (left) would likely agree that life at home wasn't as exciting as the ads (right) portrayed it.

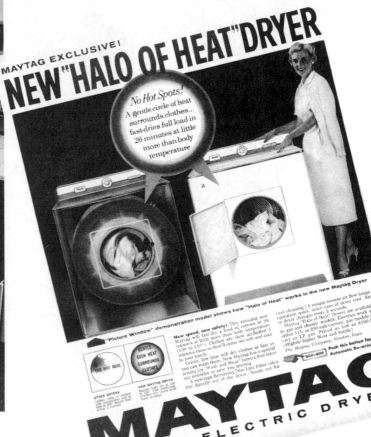

1950s Teens: Going with the Group

Comic book teen Archie Andrews dancing with his girlfriend Veronica.

Archie Andrews of Riverdale High School did not have a care in the world—other than dating Veronica and Betty and keeping his rival, Reggie, away from them. Archie and his pals were popular comic book characters. In the early 1950s, many young people seemed to act the way Archie and his friends did. It was very important, they felt, to do what the other kids did—to belong to the group. Symbols of belonging were very important. Young men—or their girlfriends—wore varsity letters on their jackets with a great feeling of pride.

During the Depression and the war years, young people did not have much time to be part of a "group." Life was too hard. But that was not the case with the children of the Baby Boom. The Baby Boomers were a lucky generation. They did not grow up with unemployment or war. And, like no other generation before them, they had money to spend on themselves. By 1959, teenagers were spending $75 million a year on popular records. Teenage girls were spending $40 million on lipstick and $837 million on school clothes.

What was important to 1950s teens? Hot rods (cars with powerful engines) and dragging (drag-strip racing) were "hip" or "cool." Dances called *sock hops* were a place to find romance. So was the malt shop or some other local "hangout" where teens spent time together. The high school, with its sports and other activities, was the center of most teen life.

The Archie-type kids were not the only kind of 1950s teens. There were also teens who were unhappy and caused trouble. Crimes by young people increased greatly in the 1950s. Between 1948 and 1953, these crimes—many of them violent—went up by 45 percent. More and more

Teenagers hanging out in a diner in 1956.

1950s Slang

Can you figure out this conversation?

"Hey, Bobby Sue, did you hear about Bugsy?"

"No, Dee Dee. What cooks?"

"Patti's got him all shook up because she took a joyride in Hank's hot rod."

"That ugly Edsel? How does Bugsy think that a chick like Patti's going to make the scene with a greaser like Hank?"

"Alex saw them. He's hip to all that jazz. He saw them cruisin' the strip in his wheels and then boppin' over to the sock hop. She's even wearing his leather jacket."

"Well, Patti better get with it, because there's Bugsy driving by right now on his way to the passion pit, with some new chick in his funky '57 Chevy"!

What did they say?

Bobby Sue and Dee Dee are talking about Bugsy, who is shocked that Patti would leave him for a boy with a leather jacket and greased hair. Patti and this boy go to a dance place together. Bugsy gets revenge by going to the drive-in movie with someone else.

Any questions?

youths joined gangs. Motorcycle gangs appeared. Gang members shared a dangerous lifestyle filled with drugs, alcohol, and violence.

Many adults said that rock 'n' roll music and movies for the young were to blame. They claimed that teen idols like rock 'n' roll singer Elvis Presley and actor James Dean steered teens toward alcohol and drug abuse. Some adults wondered whether too *much* money was actually hurting the young. In the 1950s, many parents began to wonder where they had "gone wrong." ∎

Crimes by young people went up by 45% between 1948 and 1953.

Movie musicals such as Grease *and* West Side Story *show some of the group identities of 1950s teenagers. Do you think teens have a group identity today? How do they define this identity? What are the symbols of today's young generation? How do they dress? What fads do they seem to enjoy?*

THEN & NOW

What magazine were teachers most likely to take from students in 1950s high school study halls? *Mad* magazine, of course – the magazine adults loved to hate.

Mad began in 1952. At first, it made fun of comic strips. Gradually, the magazine began to make fun of other parts of American life – as well as popular movies and TV shows. *Mad* laughed at people in charge, and that made *adults* mad. They called the magazine "trash." They wondered why their kids were reading it instead of more serious books. Some parents actually thought *Mad* was teaching bad ideas to the young.

Mad is still around today, and it is still successful. But somehow it doesn't make people angry anymore. Why not? For one thing, today's young people can see even wilder comedy, such as "Saturday Night Live" and cable TV comedians. And Bart Simpson is worse than *Mad*'s gap-toothed Alfred E. Neuman ever was. But the main reason adults put up with *Mad* these days may be this simple: today's adults were yesterday's kids – and they still enjoy reading *Mad*.

The Beat Generation

Allen Ginsberg (right) was one of the most famous of the "Beat" poets. Here, he poses with fellow poet Peter Orlovsky in Paris in 1956.

"**I** saw the best minds of my generation destroyed by madness. . . ." So wrote poet Allen Ginsberg in his poem *Howl* in the early 1950s. Ginsberg was a member of the "Beat" movement. The beats—often called *beatniks*—did *not* choose to fit in with common ways of thinking and acting in the 1950s. In the 1950s, many people tried to conform to the group; the beatniks were people who did not want to conform.

Beatniks separated themselves from the larger society. They did not have regular jobs; some wandered the countryside doing odd jobs for money. Most of them did not believe in marriage. Many used drugs. Beatniks did not want to become part of what they called "the system." They didn't want the good job, the house in the suburbs, and the security that most people desired. They thought that all of these things were part of an insane world—a world that included the threat of the nuclear bomb.

Beatniks often got together in coffeehouses to talk, read poetry, and play music. Male beatniks often had beards and wore informal clothes such as turtleneck shirts and jeans. Female beatniks wore dark, loose-fitting clothing, had long, straight hair, and wore no makeup.

For all their talk of nonconformity, beatniks themselves tended to conform within their own group, especially in their ways of dressing and talking. And they were never more than a small minority of the nation's young people. But they were an important sign that not everyone believed in "the system." They were also a sign of things to come: the more "open" 1960s. ■

America Plugs In... to Television!

A mother watching TV with her children in 1955. The number of American homes with TV sets grew from 3.9 million in 1950 to nearly 46 million by 1960.

"**A**ll I know about television," said comedian Bob Hope in the late 1940s, "is, I want to get into it as soon as possible." Ordinary Americans seemed to feel the same way. *They* wanted to "get into" television too. From 1950 to 1952, the number of American homes with TV sets grew from 3.9 million to 15 million. By 1960, there were nearly 46 million!

In the 1950s, some people thought TV would be bad for Americans. Would children who spent hours sitting in front of the TV set get enough exercise? Would families grow apart because they watched TV instead of talking? Would people stop going to see plays and sports events? These objections to TV didn't seem to matter. Harmful or not, TV was here to stay. As radio host Alistair Cooke put it in 1949, "Television is going to be a part of our world. And people who try to ignore it, or preach against it, or keep their children away from it, are soon going to show up as 'nutty' people. . . . We are doomed – or privileged, according to your point of view – to be the television generation."

Alistair Cooke was right. The Baby Boomers who grew up in the 1950s and 1960s had a new influence in their lives: television.

Who's on Tonight?

Who were the TV stars of the 1950s? Many radio stars – including Jack Benny, Ed Wynn, and George Burns – made a quick and easy switch to television. In fact, TV let these funny people do things they couldn't do on radio. On radio, no one could see Jack Benny's shrug, Ed Wynn's funny faces, or George Burns's rolling eyes. But audiences watching them on TV roared with laughter.

TV created new stars too. Among the first was Milton Berle. His "Texaco Star Theater" started in 1948. It was such a hit that the owners of stores and movie theaters said business was bad on Tuesday nights. Why? Everybody was at home watching "Uncle Miltie" tell jokes, dress up as a woman, or bring old comedy skits back to life.

Ed Sullivan's show, "Toast of the Town" (later to become "The Ed Sullivan Show"), was the first great variety show. During its 23-year run, it showed just about every kind of entertainment: comedians, Russian ballet dancers, circus acts, trained chimpanzees, opera stars, puppets, and the latest rock 'n' roll stars. When Ed

Ed Sullivan's show helped boost the careers of many performers, including Elvis Presley. The show ran for 23 years.

A scene from "The Honeymooners," in which Jackie Gleason (center) played Brooklyn bus driver Ralph Kramden.

Sullivan called Elvis Presley "a fine boy" after Elvis sang on the show, thousands of American teenagers turned to their parents and said, "See? Elvis is OK – *Ed Sullivan* said so."

TV audiences fell in love with an interesting collection of new faces during the 1950s:

• On "The Honeymooners," comedian Jackie Gleason played Brooklyn bus driver Ralph Kramden, a man with a get-rich-quick scheme up *both* his sleeves. Gleason was a master of physical comedy and the "slow burn" – quietly getting angry and then exploding.

• Jack Webb was popular as the serious police investigator of "Dragnet." The no-nonsense cop was famous for saying "Just the facts, ma'am" to chatty female witnesses.

• As the first host of the "Tonight" show, Steve Allen had a specialty: nutty comedy. He once stuck 1,000 tea bags to his body and was dunked by a crane into a tank of hot water.

• Sid Caesar and Imogene Coca were the very funny stars of "Your Show of Shows." From 1950 through 1954, this program gave Americans 90 minutes of new comedy each week. Some of the show's writers became famous in later years: Neil Simon as a playwright, Mel Brooks and Woody Allen as writers and directors of movie comedies.

• Radio journalist Edward R. Murrow made the change to TV. He interviewed politicians, movie stars, and other famous people on "See It Now" and "Person to Person." The deep-voiced Murrow became America's most trusted TV journalist.

And Now, a Word from Our Sponsor . . .

Oh, we're the men from Texaco
We work from Maine to Mexico
There's nothing like this Texaco
    of ours . . .

The Texaco Service Men, four singers dressed as gas station attendants for Texaco, an oil company, opened Milton Berle's show. Many older Americans can still sing that advertising jingle.

In TV commercials of the 1950s, men were men and women were . . . well, housewives. It was a sign of the times. "Welcome to a *man's* world," said a deep-voiced announcer in a commercial for pipe tobacco. Other ads for men's products featured hunters, race car drivers, and baseball players. Women in commercials were usually at home – showing other women better ways to cook dinner, wash clothes, or wax the floor.

Early TV ads often used a spokesperson for the product. Singer Dinah Shore told us to "See the U.S.A. in your Chevrolet." Newsman John Cameron Swayze put Timex watches through many "torture tests" to show that the watches were waterproof and sturdy. (Once, a stuntman wore a Timex during a high dive. Another time, a Timex was tied to the front of a speedboat.) "It takes a licking, but it keeps on ticking!" Swayze always said.

Sometimes, the spokesperson wasn't a person at all. Speedy Alka-Seltzer, a cartoon doll, told viewers how Alka-Seltzer could take care of an upset stomach. Tony the Tiger was a cartoon character who sold Sugar Frosted Flakes, a breakfast cereal. "They're GR-R-REAT!!" he roared.

From the very earliest days of television, Americans complained about TV commercials. But like them or not, we remember them. And sometimes the tune or words of an old ad can bring back memories.

"Speedy" was seen in many Alka-Seltzer commercials during the 1950s.

For many years, children enjoyed watching "Captain Kangaroo."

• Very young children loved the gentle "Captain Kangaroo." The show starred Bob Keeshan (the captain) and his friends Mr. Green Jeans, Bunny Rabbit, and Mister Moose. "Howdy Doody," a show starring a freckle-faced puppet and a cowboy named Buffalo Bob, was another favorite.

• "The Mickey Mouse Club" made its teenage performers famous from coast to coast. Annette Funicello grew up to star in movie musicals of the early 1960s.

• TV cartoons hit a high point with "Rocky and His Friends." The jokes on this show were as much for adults as for children. The show's bad guy was a Russian spy named Boris Badenov. Rocky's friend Bullwinkle (a moose) played football for a college called Wossamatta U.

• America loved the Old West—and James Arness became a TV hero as Marshal Matt Dillon on "Gunsmoke." Westerns had been a popular kind of movie and radio show—and they made the move to TV.

"The Mickey Mouse Club" (left) was a favorite of children. Lucille Ball and Desi Arnaz (above) starred in the extremely popular "I Love Lucy" comedy show.

Everybody Loved Lucy

Late in 1951, comedian Lucille Ball went on the air as the redheaded wife of a Cuban bandleader. The show was "I Love Lucy." It was an instant hit. TV experts estimate that near the end of its first season, 11 million TV sets were tuned to "Lucy" every Monday night. At the time, there were only 15 million sets in American homes!

The plots of "I Love Lucy" were simple. Every week, Lucy got herself into some kind of comic trouble. Then she was found out by her husband, Ricky (played by real-life husband Desi

Arnaz). "Lucy, you got some 'splainin' [explaining] to do!" he would shout.

Why did people love Lucy? Part of the reason was that Lucy was not a fool. Audiences could laugh *with* her more than *at* her. "Lucy was not stupid," writes TV historian Rick Marschall, ". . . but she was childlike. She took childlike delight in [planning] an innocent trick. She pleaded with Ricky to meet a celebrity as a child would plead. . . . There is a fine line in comedy between childlike and childish, and Lucille Ball—like Laurel and Hardy before her—had the magic touch." ■

> **"There is a fine line in comedy between childlike and childish, and Lucille Ball . . . had the magic touch."**

Some people think children spend too much time watching TV. What do you think? In what ways is TV good for kids? In what ways is it bad for them?

Many libraries and video stores carry tapes of "The Honeymooners," "Dragnet," "I Love Lucy," and other 1950s TV shows. Rent tapes like these to see what 1950s TV was like.

Do you think that commercials influence what you buy? If not, what does influence what you buy? Some people think that commercials focus too much on being young, sexy, good-looking, and rich. What do you think? Do commercials teach false values to children and adults?

THEN & NOW

Soap operas easily made the move from radio to TV. Actually, they were called daytime dramas or serials. But they were nicknamed *soap operas* because they were filled with emotion, like operas, and often were sponsored by companies that made soap.

At first, soap opera episodes were 15 minutes long. But soon, they were half-hour programs. Usually shown every weekday, they told continuing stories about the problems of their characters. Most often, they were about families. Some of the most popular shows in the 1950s were "Search for Tomorrow," "Love of Life," and "The Secret Storm." One of the most realistic began in 1956: "As the World Turns" was still running in the 1990s.

Soap operas are still a big part of TV's afternoon schedule. But the 1990s "soaps" are different in some ways from the shows of the 1950s. For one thing, there is more sex in them. Soaps have followed changes in morality and new standards for what can be said and shown on TV. Also, unlike the "bad" characters in the 1950s, today's bad characters often get away with their deeds. For example, Erica Kane often comes out a winner on "All My Children." Another difference: 1990s characters are often glamorous and rich. People today seem to enjoy seeing rich lifestyles and expensive clothes.

In spite of all these differences, however, one thing remains the same: the reason that people watch soap operas. We get hooked on soaps because they are about people. As silly as soaps sometimes are, they show problems we can understand and think about. And besides, who *doesn't* like to look into other people's lives?

THE ROCK 'N' ROLL REVOLUTION

Dick Clark's show, "American Bandstand" (top) featured the latest rock 'n' roll songs and dances. Chuck Berry (bottom) was one of the first rock musicians.

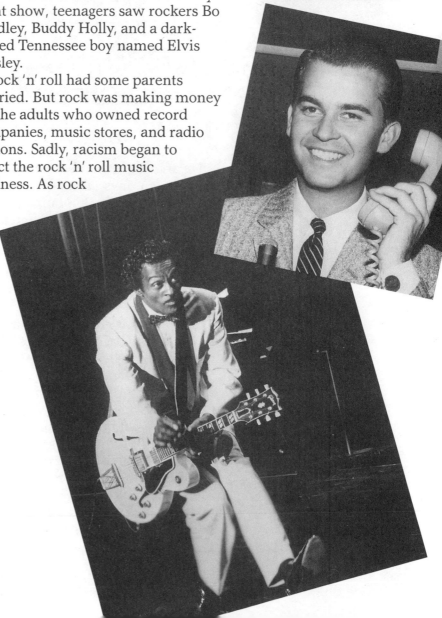

"Rock 'n' roll is here to stay," sang Danny and the Juniors back in the late 1950s. They were right. Rock *was* here to stay. Although the "older generation" was still dancing to the Big Band sound, teenagers of the 1950s were dancing to a new beat.

A new kind of music called *rock 'n' roll* was the "in" sound for America's young people. Rock 'n' roll was a mix of jazz, swing, country music, and—most of all—the black American music called *rhythm and blues*. Sometimes it was hard to understand the words behind the loud guitars in rock 'n' roll songs. But the words didn't matter much. What mattered was the *beat*— the loud, driving rhythm of the music.

What did American teenagers like best about rock 'n' roll? Maybe they liked the fact that it made their parents nervous. Adults worried that rock music was too wild, too sexy. Legendary rock singer Chuck Berry remembers his church-going family telling him, "You'd better not be singing no devil's music!" But he adds, "My first record was a hit, and when $800 came in everybody said, 'A-*men*!' "

Rock music was everywhere. A 1955 movie about inner-city teenagers, *The Blackboard Jungle*, began with an ear-blasting version of the song "Rock Around the Clock." After school, teenagers across the country watched "American Bandstand" to hear the latest singing groups and see the newest dances. And on Ed Sullivan's Sunday night show, teenagers saw rockers Bo Diddley, Buddy Holly, and a dark-haired Tennessee boy named Elvis Presley.

Rock 'n' roll had some parents worried. But rock was making money for the adults who owned record companies, music stores, and radio stations. Sadly, racism began to affect the rock 'n' roll music business. As rock

music was taken over by the recording industry, stations played fewer original rock hits sung by black performers. Instead, the music business played a white singer's remake of the original hit song.

In the 1960s, rock music would become the music of protest. But in the 1950s, rock was all about being young, happy, full of life – and looking for love. In the words of a hit song, it made American teenagers want to "SHOUT!" ■

Why did parents in the 1950s dislike rock 'n' roll music so much? Is there any kind of music today that young people like and parents hate? Is rap music today anything like rock 'n' roll was in the 1950s? What do you think of rap?

Elvis Presley arrived on the music scene "like an explosion."

The King

He arrived, remembers singer Waylon Jennings, "like an explosion." Singer Bob Luman remembers: "This cat came out in red pants and a green coat and a pink shirt and socks, and he had this sneer on his face and he stood behind the mike for five minutes, I'll bet, before he made a move. Then he hit his guitar a lick, and he broke two strings. . . . These high school girls were screaming and fainting and running up to the stage. . . . He made chills run up my back, man, like when your hair starts grabbing at your collar."

That was "the king" of rock 'n' roll, Elvis Presley. Raised in Memphis, Tennessee, Elvis grew up listening to gospel and country music on the radio. In the clubs down on Beale Street, he heard black blues singers.

In the summer of 1954, the teenage Elvis met Memphis record producer Sam Phillips. A woman who worked for Phillips recalled, "I remember Sam saying, 'If I could find a white man who had the Negro sound and the Negro feel, I could make a billion dollars.' " When he heard Elvis, Phillips knew he was on to something big.

Why do Americans still listen to early Elvis songs like "That's All Right," "Jailhouse Rock," "Heartbreak Hotel," "Blue Suede Shoes," "Return to Sender," and "Don't Be Cruel"? Because they know that the young Elvis Presley was – and still *is* – the spirit of rock 'n' roll.

Hollywood Meets Television

At the end of World War II, 82 million Americans went to the movies every week. But by the early 1950s, that number had dropped sharply—to only 36 million. What had happened? In a word: *television*.

The American public wanted to stay home. They'd gone all over the world to fight the war. Now, they were buying houses in the suburbs, and it was a long drive back to the old movie theaters downtown. Besides, they didn't need to go to the movies; they could watch TV.

How could Hollywood compete with this fascinating new "toy" called television? By finding ways to do things TV *couldn't* do. In 1950s Hollywood, the focus was on the *S* words: sex, size, and spectacle.

Sex was something the movies could do bigger and better than television. Because TV shows were shown in people's homes, they had to be "clean" enough for family viewing. So during the 1950s, American movie sex got steamier—in movies like *From Here to Eternity* and *Peyton Place*. Director Alfred Hitchcock made sexy thrillers (*Vertigo*, *North by Northwest*, and *Rear Window*). And a mix of teenage sex and rebellion drew young audiences to movies like *Rebel Without a Cause* and *The Wild One*.

New Movie Technology

Early TV pictures were often small and blurry, and always black and white. The movies could do better, and in the 1950s breakthroughs like Technicolor and CinemaScope changed their look. Moviemakers hoped making movies bigger, wider, more colorful (and even three-dimensional) would pull large numbers of Americans off of their sofas . . . and back to the movie theaters.

With the coming of wide-screen techniques such as Cinerama and CinemaScope, movie screens got bigger. Movie audiences were supposed to feel as though they were inside the movie, not just watching it. That was the idea behind 3-D (three-dimensional) movies too. Moviegoers wore special glasses to watch the movie. Trains would seem to race toward them. Monsters would seem to reach out from the screen. 3-D was exciting, but it didn't work very well. Moviemakers eventually dropped it.

Marilyn Monroe, shown here in a scene from *The Seven Year Itch*, was a sex symbol of the 1950s.

A movie audience (top) wears special "3-D" glasses. James Dean (center) was a hero to rebellious teens. Cary Grant (right) with Eva Marie Saint in Alfred Hitchcock's *North by Northwest*.

Color and music made movies bigger and better too. After the black-and-white movies of wartime years, Hollywood went back to making most of its movies in color. (TV shows were shown in black and white.) Hollywood composers wrote music for historical films such as *The Ten Commandments*, *The Big Country*, and *Ben-Hur*. Musicals also filled the wide screen. *An American in Paris*, *The Band Wagon*, *Seven Brides for Seven Brothers*, and *A Star Is Born* brought exciting new music to theaters. The small TV sets of the 1950s couldn't match the sound of music in a movie theater.

The "Little" Movies

Of course, not every movie was a wide-screen epic. Movie studios and new independent moviemakers looked for ways to make good "little" movies too. Among their success stories were:
• Low-budget monster, horror, and outer-space movies: *I Was a Teen-age Werewolf*, *Attack of the 50 Ft. Woman*, *Them*, *House of Wax*, *Forbidden Planet*, and others. Among the best was

Invasion of the Body Snatchers. The plot? Outer-space creatures steal people, putting alien "fakes" in their place. Many people saw the movie as a takeoff on the 1950s fear of being taken over by Communist spies.

• Black-and-white movies about gangsters, detectives, and life on the edge of American society. Among the best of the *film noir* ("dark movie") style were *Body and Soul*, *White Heat*, *The Asphalt Jungle*, and *The Naked City*.

• "Social issue" movies that got people talking about America's problems: prejudice (*12 Angry Men* and *Gentleman's Agreement*), corrupt labor unions (*On the Waterfront*), and problem teenagers (*The Blackboard Jungle*). ■

The article describes how the movie industry met the challenge of TV in the 1950s. Now, Hollywood must meet another challenge—home video viewing.

Many people rarely go to movie theaters nowadays. They rent movies to watch at home instead. Which do you prefer: renting or going to a theater? Why?

Imagine that you have been hired by a movie theater owner to create ads convincing people to come to the theater. What reasons would you include in your ad campaign? What can the theater offer that watching at home can't offer?

Have you seen any of the 1950s movies mentioned in the article? Consider renting one or two that sound interesting to you.

THEN & NOW

In the 1950s, the movie industry faced new competition: the television networks. Today, the TV networks are the ones being challenged. The two new competitors are cable TV and home videos.

In the early 1990s, nearly six out of 10 American homes had cable TV. The growing popularity of cable has taken away much of the TV networks' audience. In the mid-1970s, the "big three" networks (CBS, NBC, and ABC) had 95 percent of the nation's TV audience. By 1989, they had only 60 percent—an all-time low.

The other new competitor is home videos. In 1975, Sony introduced the first videocassette recorder (VCR) to the United States. The networks protested. They said it wasn't fair for people to be able to tape network TV shows and watch them again and again for free. The networks took their case to court, but they lost. The Supreme Court refused to ban or limit VCRs. By 1989, 65 percent of American homes had a VCR, and viewers could not only tape TV shows, but also choose from 40,000 movie titles to rent or buy.

Still, the networks are surviving the new challenges. Even though they have more competition, there are plenty of viewers for everyone in a country with 92 million TV sets. And Americans are watching more TV than ever—over *seven hours* a day on the average.

The movie industry is doing well too. Even though movies can be seen on cable and videocassette, theater admissions topped 1 billion for the 13th straight year in 1989. Americans still like the big screen.

Explosion of Words

When paperbacks became widely available after World War II, buyers had a new source of inexpensive books.

One of the bestselling books of the 1950s was Dr. Benjamin Spock's "bible" for parents, *Baby and Child Care*. Americans wanted to raise happy, healthy children. Here was a "how-to" book that seemed to hold the key.

Serious fiction writers were telling a different story. They were talking about the flaws and problems of the American Dream of success — the dream parents were raising their children to achieve.

Ex-soldiers Norman Mailer (*The Naked and the Dead*) and James Jones (*From Here to Eternity*) wrote novels about the still-fresh World War II experience. In different ways, each of them saw war as a kind of American big business. Jones's book takes place before the attack on Pearl Harbor. The career soldiers want to be promoted — just like any company's employees. They see the coming war as a way to move up in the world — a way to reach their American Dream.

Other writers began to dig into the problems of racism and prejudice in the United States. African-American writers James Baldwin (*Go Tell It on the Mountain*) and Ralph Ellison (*Invisible Man*) wrote about the lives of black Americans. These books reached a large white audience. In much the same way, black playwright Lorraine Hansberry's play *A Raisin in the Sun* was a breakthrough. It made white theater audiences think about black characters and their problems.

What was the American Dream doing to us? Novelist Sloan Wilson's *The Man in the Gray Flannel Suit* described an ex-soldier now working for a giant corporation. He decides that the price of success is too high. In the end, Tom Rath decides to put his personal life and family *ahead* of his job. This was a new idea to many people in the 1950s.

Still other writers explored the problems facing young Americans. Young people were pressured to live up to their parents' dream of success. J. D. Salinger's novel *The Catcher in the Rye*

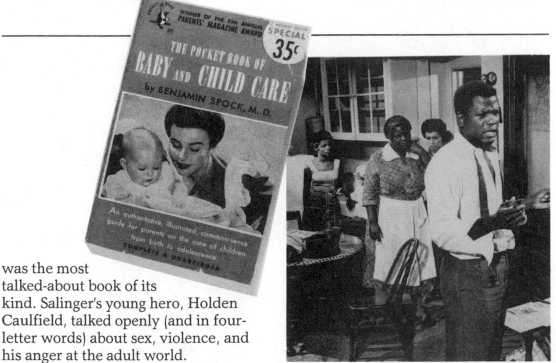

was the most talked-about book of its kind. Salinger's young hero, Holden Caulfield, talked openly (and in four-letter words) about sex, violence, and his anger at the adult world.

Critics found the book and its language "explosive . . . brilliant . . . repellent . . . appallingly funny." But America's parents didn't find it very funny. In many school districts and libraries around the country, *Catcher* was banned from the shelves and reading lists. ■

Books such as The Naked and the Dead, Invisible Man, *and* The Man in the Gray Flannel Suit *pointed out problems in American society in the 1950s. If you were to write a novel today, what problems in America would you explore? What solutions would you suggest?*

Dr. Benjamin Spock's *Baby and Child Care* (left) was a bestselling book of the 1950s. Lorraine Hansberry's play *A Raisin in the Sun* (right) made white audiences think about black life. (This scene is from the 1961 movie.)

A Raisin in the Sun: Reaching for a Dream

Lorraine Hansberry's 1958 play shows a black family reaching for a dream, which includes moving from the inner city to a middle-class neighborhood. When faced with bigoted new neighbors, they react with pride:

WALTER (*A beat. The tension hangs; then WALTER steps back from it*) Yeah. Well—what I mean is that we come from people who had a lot of *pride*. I mean—we are very proud people. And that's my sister over there and she's going to be a doctor—and we are very proud—

LINDNER Well—I am sure that is very nice, but—

WALTER What I am telling you is that we called you over here to tell you that we are very proud and that this— (*Signaling to* TRAVIS) Travis, come here. (TRAVIS *crosses and* WALTER *draws him before him facing the man*) This is my son, and he makes the sixth generation our family in this country. And we have all thought about your offer—

LINDNER Well, good . . . good—

WALTER And we have decided to move into our house because my father—my father—he earned it for us brick by brick. (MAMA *has her eyes closed and is rocking back and forth as though she were in church, with her head nodding the Amen yes*) We don't want to make no trouble for nobody or fight no causes, and we will try to be good neighbors. And that's *all* we got to say about that. (*He looks the man absolutely in the eyes*) We don't want your money. (*He turns and walks away*)

LINDNER (*Looking around at all of them*) I take it then—that you have decided to occupy . . .

BENEATHA That's what the man said.

LINDNER (*To* MAMA *in her reverie*) Then I would like to appeal to you, Mrs. Younger. You are older and wiser and understand things better I am sure . . .

Big Changes in the Old Game

Jackie Robinson broke baseball's color ban by becoming the first black player in the major leagues.

After World War II, professional baseball went through many changes. One welcome change was a big increase in the number of fans attending the games. Most of the 16 ball clubs set season attendance records in the late 1940s. The Cleveland Indians drew more than 2.6 million fans in 1948, a record that stood for more than 20 years. Baseball also began showing up on that new invention – television. But the most dramatic changes in baseball were very basic ones: who played the game and where they played.

Breaking the Color Ban

For years, the National Association for the Advancement of Colored People (NAACP) had spoken out against it. Fair-minded sportswriters and other people interested in justice had said it was wrong. What was "it"? It was an unwritten rule followed by all baseball team owners. It was baseball's color ban. Team owners did not hire black players, no matter how talented the players were. In the mid-1940s, a black man could put on a military uniform and carry a rifle—but he could not put on a major-league baseball uniform and swing a bat. According to baseball club owners, the fans would not accept black players as teammates of whites.

One baseball executive had different ideas. He was Branch Rickey, president of the Brooklyn Dodgers. Rickey decided that it was time for baseball to be integrated. He signed a black ballplayer in 1946. The man he selected, Jackie Robinson, was especially qualified to be a pioneer. First of all, he had major-league talent. But he also had other strengths. At 26 years old, he was older than most rookies. He had competed successfully with whites in several sports. He had been an army officer. Rickey felt that Robinson was mature and could control himself if people insulted him.

He would need to. Shouts of "Go home, nigger!" followed him through the minor leagues and into the majors when he began to play with the Dodgers in 1947. That year, several players threatened to go on strike rather than have Robinson in the league. Ford Frick, president of the National League, took a firm stand. He told the white players:

If you do this you will be suspended from the league. You will find that the friends you think you have in the press box will not support you, that you will be outcasts. I do not care if half the league strikes. . . . I don't care if it wrecks the National League for five years. This is the United States of America, and one citizen has as much right to play as another.

The white players heeded Frick's warning. Robinson played for the rest of the season. In silence, he took insults from the stands and other players. Wherever he played, many fans—black and white—came out to watch him.

And they liked what they saw. Robinson was a man of great courage and strength—and he was also a great player. As the Dodgers' second baseman, he proved immediately that he belonged. He was a powerful hitter, a quick runner, and a steady fielder. Robinson played so well that he was voted Rookie of the Year in 1947. Two years later, he was voted the Most Valuable Player (MVP) in the National League.

Jackie Robinson (left) signing a professional contract with the Brooklyn Dodgers in 1946. Dodgers' president Branch Rickey (right) fought to integrate baseball.

Mickey Mantle was a star centerfielder for the Yankees.

Black players also began to arrive in the American League. Larry Doby was the first. In 1948, 42-year-old Satchel Paige was signed by the Cleveland Indians in time to help them win the American League pennant and the World Series.

With these examples to inspire them, other blacks followed. Many became instant stars. Through 1959, nine Rookies of the Year and eight MVPs were African-Americans. By the late 1950s, there were black players on every team. Many, including Robinson, were eventually voted into baseball's Hall of Fame.

On the Move

Pittsburgh. Cincinnati. Detroit. Washington, D.C. Cleveland. Two each in Boston, St. Louis, Philadelphia, and Chicago. And three in New York.

These were the stars of the

New York's Golden Age

The Dodgers and Giants left New York City for the West Coast after the 1957 baseball season. So the nation's largest city was suddenly left with only one major-league team—the New York Yankees (until 1962, when the National League added the New York Mets). But New Yorkers could be proud of their last years with three teams. No city had ever dominated a sport as New York had dominated baseball in the late 1940s and 1950s. In the nine years from 1949 through 1957, the World Series had matched either the Yankees and Dodgers or the Yankees and Giants *six* times. At least one New York team appeared in every series from 1949 through

1958. Only once did a team from another city *win* the series: in 1957, the Milwaukee Braves beat the Yankees.

In the 1950s, New York also had baseball's most glamorous players. There was Jackie Robinson. And each team was graced by a superb centerfielder: the Dodgers' Duke Snider, the Yankees' Mickey Mantle, and the Giants' Willie Mays. Many a New York argument broke out over which player was best.

Fans outside of New York could only shake their heads—and enjoy seeing the New York teams visit their cities. And they could do what fans do everywhere—wait. Things would change.

century. Until the 1950s, these were the cities in which major-league baseball was played. Suddenly, that changed.

Why did baseball team owners start moving their teams in the 1950s? Like other business leaders, they went where the money was. More and more people were living in growing cities in the South, the West, and the Midwest. They wanted – and were willing to pay for – major-league sports. At the same time, jet airplanes made it possible for teams to fly across the country to play ball games. Owners, especially those whose teams were struggling, were tempted to leave their old homes.

The National League's Boston Braves were the first to go. Never as popular in Boston as the American League Red Sox, the Braves moved to new territory – Milwaukee, Wisconsin – in 1953. The St. Louis Browns became the Baltimore Orioles the next year. A year later, the Philadelphia Athletics resettled in Kansas City.

These moves bothered many fans, but what came next shocked them. New York's two National League teams, the New York Giants and the Brooklyn Dodgers, were two of the most successful and colorful teams in sports. After the 1957 season, the two announced that the rumors were true: next season, they would become the San Francisco Giants and Los Angeles Dodgers. Baseball fans felt as though the stars in the night sky were shifting. It was a time of genuine sadness in New York. At the last New York Giants game, a fan carried a sad banner. It said, "STAY TEAM STAY," a heartbroken twist on the old battle cry "GO TEAM GO."

But the Giants didn't stay. Along with the Dodgers, they went west – to start a new era in baseball. ■

Why do you think baseball became integrated in 1947? Why might the time have been "right" then – instead of earlier? How do you think integration changed the game of baseball?

These fans (left) don't want the Giants to leave New York. But in the 1958 season, the Giants began playing in San Francisco.

The **NBA** Is Born

In one way, basketball is the only truly American sport. It did not grow out of older European games as baseball and football did. It was invented by Massachusetts college professor James Naismith in 1891 as an indoor winter sport. In the early 20th century, it became popular as a high school and college sport.

But until the postwar era, professional basketball was not solid. A professional could play in one of several leagues. Or he could play on a "barnstorming" team, which arranged its own games. These teams often went out of business.

In 1949, the two biggest leagues signed an agreement to form one league – the National Basketball Association (NBA). It was a grand name, but a shaky league. Teams of very different skill levels and financial health had been thrown together. Would the NBA succeed?

Star Power

The new NBA, with teams from New York to Denver, had one thing going for it – it already had many famous players. None was more popular than George Mikan. At 6'10", Mikan was the first of the big centers in the pro game. In February 1950, he was named "greatest basketball player of the last 50 years" by the Associated Press. Mikan wore glasses that made him look like a professor. His looks reminded some that Mikan had once studied to be a priest. But he did not play like a priest. He didn't care whom he had to push aside to get to the ball.

In 1950, Mikan's Minneapolis Lakers won the first NBA championship over the Syracuse Nationals, a team with a star of its own – Dolph Schayes. Schayes was known for his two-handed over-the-head set shot. He also excelled in tough play. "We were all battlers," he recalls. "You begin to think that way and your whole personality changes."

Keys to Success

One key to the success of the NBA was its willingness to adjust. Teams that could not make the grade were dropped. League officials also changed some rules to create more action. In one change, teams had to shoot the ball within 24 seconds of getting it. This prevented stalling and encouraged more scoring. To keep players from hurting each other, the league added special foul rules.

In the meantime, great players kept signing onto strong and popular teams.

Neil Johnston, Paul Arizin, and Tom Gola turned the Philadelphia Warriors into a threat. Bob Pettit starred for the St. Louis Hawks. Two Olympic stars – Ralph Beard and Alex Groza – led the Indianapolis Olympians. Many African-Americans joined the league during the 1950s. The Boston Celtics signed Chuck Cooper; the New York Knicks signed Sweetwater Clifton. By the end of the 1950s, the NBA had such outstanding black players as Elgin Baylor and Wilt Chamberlain.

George Mikan was the first of the big centers in pro basketball. He led the Minneapolis Lakers to five NBA titles in their first six seasons.

him. And then when you were ready to shoot he would come up and hit the ball some kind of way.

In 1960, the Celtics won their third championship in four years. They set a standard for everyone else to follow. With a defensive ace in Russell, a great passer in Cousy, and a fast style of play, the Celtics showed that success was the result of skill and coaching, not just power. ■

THEN & NOW

On April 23, 1950, the Minneapolis Lakers defeated the Syracuse Nationals to win the first NBA championship. A crowd of more than 9,000 watched the contest in Minneapolis. The game was reported in the newspapers. But few people could have guessed that in 40 years this young professional league would grow into a monster—an equal of major-league baseball and the National Football League.

In the 1989-90 season, more than 15 million fans attended regular-season games. Millions more watched the NBA on television. Results of championship games appeared on the front pages of newspapers and in major sports magazines. Instead of the original 62 to 68 games, each team played 82 games. The season now covered nine months, and the championship game was played in late June. Superstars Magic Johnson and Michael Jordan each earned more than $3 million per year in salary. They earned millions more in product endorsements.

K.C. Jones (left) joined the Boston Celtics in 1958. The Celtics won eight straight titles with Jones as a player. In the 1980s, they won two titles with Jones as their head coach.

Celtics Triumphant

But one black player, Bill Russell, made the biggest contribution of all. He joined the Boston Celtics in 1956. By that time, coach Red Auerbach had grouped some of the finest stars in the game. Bob Cousy, Tom Heinsohn, and Bill Sharman needed just one new teammate—a center. Russell turned out to be that player. He was tremendous at rebounding and shot blocking. Sweetwater Clifton remembers what it was like playing against Russell:

All Russell did was stand back under the basket, you understand, and wait for the player to come to

Golf Catches On

Every decade has its images— pictures that seem to define the time. One such image in the 1950s was President Dwight Eisenhower playing golf. On TV, in newsreels, and in newspapers and magazines, a white-capped Eisenhower was pictured teeing off. "Ike" was a popular president, and he helped make golf popular in the United States. In earlier years, "following that little white ball around" was thought to be a game for the upper class. In the 1950s, the middle class began to play golf. Golf was especially popular in the wide-open spaces of the new suburbs. A weekend round of golf was part of the suburban "good life."

Two Great Pros

At the same time, golf professionals were attracting fans to the game. One of the first great postwar champions was a Texan, Ben Hogan. Hogan won 37 tournaments from 1945 through 1948. In 1948, he won both the U.S. Open and the PGA Championship, two of golf's four major tournaments. His goal in 1949 was to win the other two major matches—the Masters and the British Open. But in February, his car collided with a bus. Hogan was seriously hurt. No one thought that he would walk again—much less play competitive golf. One year later, however, Ben Hogan was back again, playing better than ever. He continued to win major tournaments through the early 1950s.

Another inspiring golfer arrived on the scene in 1954: Arnold Palmer. He won the U.S. Amateur trophy. After he became a pro, he won the Masters in 1958; he won both the Masters and the

U.S. Open in 1960. These achievements were impressive. But it was his bold style of play that made him the most popular golfer of all time. His fans, sometimes called "Arnie's Army," were thrilled to see him take risky shots rather than play it safe.

More than any other player, Palmer turned golf into a national sport that many fans watched. His popularity also helped increase the prize money available to tournament winners. ∎

President Eisenhower teeing off in a round of golf. "Ike" helped make golf popular in the United States.

Tennis, Everyone?

Tennis was a game for the rich in the early 20th century. Courts were found mainly at posh country clubs. But after World War II, people had more time and money and more places to play. Courts sprang up in suburban parks and city playlots.

In San Diego, Maureen Connolly took up tennis after watching people play at the public courts near her home. With the help of local professional players, she developed her natural talent so quickly that she won the U.S. Open at age 16, in 1951. The following year, "Little Mo" won both the U.S. Open and Wimbledon. In 1953, she became the first woman to capture the "Grand Slam" by winning all four major tennis competitions—the Australian, French, and U.S. Opens and Wimbledon. She won two more major tournaments the following year. She certainly would have stayed at the top, but a horseback-riding injury forced her to retire at age 19.

There were other signs that tennis was now a game for all Americans. A black woman, Althea Gibson, rose to the top of the game in the 1950s. Born on a cotton farm in Silver, South Carolina, Althea moved to Harlem in New York City when she was three years old. Gibson learned tennis in a program run by the police department. And she learned to play hard. "When she hits a ball," wrote a *New York Times* reporter, "it travels like a bolt out of a crossbow."

As a black, she was not always greeted warmly. She suffered some of the same abuse Jackie Robinson faced. But she had the support of fellow athletes. In 1950, there were rumors that Gibson would not be allowed to compete in the U.S. Open. Former tennis great Alice Marble wrote a guest editorial for *American Lawn Tennis Magazine*. If Gibson was not given a chance to play, Marble wrote, "then there is a . . . mark against a game to which I have devoted most of my life, and I would be bitterly ashamed." Gibson did play in that and other major tournaments. In 1956, she captured the French Open. In 1957 and 1958, she took both Wimbledon and the U.S. Open. Returning home to New York after her first Wimbledon triumph, Gibson was greeted by a ticker-tape parade. ■

Althea Gibson (bottom) playing at Wimbledon in 1956. Maureen Connolly (right) holding the trophy she won at the 1954 International Tennis Tournament in Rome, Italy.

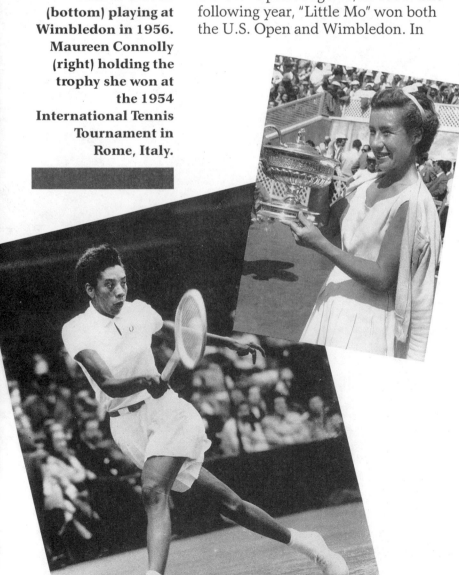

Boxing at Its Peak

Sportswriter Red Smith once said that boxing is "one of the purest of art forms." If this is true, then the years from the end of the war through the 1950s were one long art festival. Some of the greatest talents that ever stepped into the ring were on display.

Great Boxers

Perhaps the best of all the ring artists was Sugar Ray Robinson. Writer W. C. Heinz called him the "greatest fighter pound-for-pound and punch-for-punch" in 50 years. He held the welterweight crown from 1946 until 1951. In 1951, he knocked out Jake "Raging Bull" LaMotta for the middleweight title. Later on in the decade, he lost and won back the crown four times! He almost won the light-heavyweight title from a much heavier Joey Maxim, but heat exhaustion got to him. That evening was so hot that the referee had to be replaced. When he retired in 1965, Sugar Ray had won 175 out of 202 professional prizefights.

The postwar period was also the time of Rocky Marciano, who was heavyweight champion from 1952 to 1955. He retired after 49 pro fights — undefeated. The next champ was young Floyd Patterson, one of the many Olympic winners to make it as a professional.

Great Rivalries

In the late 1940s and early 1950s, middleweights Tony Zale and Rocky Graziano fought three spectacular bouts. Rocky won the second of these battles. After the fight, he said over the radio, "Hey, Ma — your bad boy done it. I told you somebody up there likes me."

In the featherweight division, Willy Pep and Sandy Saddler waged war. Unusually tall for a featherweight, Saddler was described by writer A. J. Liebling as "a bundle of loosely joined fishing poles, but they are apparently pickled bamboo; he takes a good punch, and his thin arms and legs never seem to tire." Despite the two men's skill, their last fight in 1951 was one of the dirtiest championships ever. "By some oversight," wrote James P. Dawson in the *New York Times*, "they failed to bite each other." They didn't fail to pinch, gouge, and strangle. Both were suspended. ■

Sugar Ray Robinson (right) in action against Kid Gavilan in 1949.

Olympic Report

World War II had canceled the 1940 and 1944 Olympics. As a result, the world welcomed the 1948 games. It was as if "the sun had come out," according to runner Emil Zátopek of Czechoslovakia.

The United States won the most medals that year, including a gold medal for its basketball team. On the squad was Donald Barksdale, the first black to play on an American Olympic basketball team.

Two Tense Olympics

The 1952 summer games in Helsinki marked the Soviet Union's first entrance in the Olympics since 1912. Tension between Communist and non-Communist nations was everywhere. American decathlon winner Bob Mathias said of the Soviets: "They were in a sense the real enemy. You just had to beat 'em."

Overall, the United States took home most of the medals in 1952. U.S. athletes did extremely well in the throwing contests. They broke three Olympic records: Parry O'Brien in shot put, Sam Iness in discus, and Cy Young in javelin.

Wilma Rudolph winning the women's 200 meters in the 1960 Olympics.

In the 1956 Olympics at Melbourne, Australia, East-West relations were no better. Memories of Soviet violence against the 1956 Hungarian uprising were still fresh. In a water polo match between Hungary and Russia, fights broke out and bloodied the pool. The match had to be stopped.

American athletes performed well in 1956. American diver Pat McCormick won two gold medals in diving. In track, Bobby Morrow became the first man since Jesse Owens to win both the 100- and the 200-meter dashes. Tom Courtney set an Olympic record in the 800 meters. Parry O'Brien and Al Oerter set records in the shot put and discus. But the Soviet Union captured most of the medals. Gymnast Larissa Latynina won two gold and two silver medals. This remarkable athlete competed in two more Olympics, winning a total of 18 medals!

American Victories in Rome

The USSR took home 103 medals from the 1960 Olympics in Rome, Italy. Coming in second place was the United States, with 71 medals.

For the United States, Wilma Rudolph, who was stricken by polio as a child, won gold medals in three running events. Lee Calhoun and Glen Davis repeated their 1956 victories in men's hurdles. Americans also won gold medals in the long jump, shot put, discus, and decathlon. Pole-vaulter Don Bragg let loose with a Tarzan yell when he won. "It echoed through the stands," he remembers, "and everybody went crazy."

Perhaps the biggest 1960 American victory of all came in basketball. The American team had so much talent that year that 10 players ended up as professionals. Future NBA star John Havlicek made the Olympic team only as an alternate. ■

Politics are not supposed to matter at the Olympics. But often, the games are affected by political issues. The cold war rivalries of the 1952 and 1956 games are just one example.

Do you think that the Olympics can ever be free from politics? Should they be?

Do you think athletes should refuse to compete against athletes from "enemy" countries?

Do you think the United States should refuse to send a team to the Olympic Games if the games are held in an "enemy" country?

Why or why not?

A Hungarian water polo player leaving the pool after a violent match with the Soviet team in the 1956 Olympics.

Peacetime Boom

"**E**verything is booming but the guns," said labor leader George Meany in the mid-1950s. It was a time of peace and prosperity for the United States. America was the richest and most powerful nation on earth.

After the Great Depression and World War II, Americans were ready to earn and spend money. America's economy was booming. From 1947 until 1960, the GNP, or gross national product (the value of all goods and services produced in the country in one year), increased by 3.5 percent a year. That's a very high figure – nearly 50 percent higher than in the early 1900s.

Why Did It Happen?

Why did America prosper after the war? Mostly because of the war itself.

Because of the war effort, factory workers had learned new skills. They wanted to use these skills to succeed in the postwar world. Also, they had earned high wages during the war. And because there was little they could buy during the war, they had saved a large part of those wages. By 1945,

Americans had saved billions of dollars. They were ready to buy the products that factories were turning out.

What's more, many other countries had been hit hard by the war. Those countries needed the goods the United States could produce. In addition, new ideas for making things had been developed during the war. Now those ideas could be put into practice.

Happy—
Happy—
Happy
Meals!

Yes, happy meals—the whole family loves the better *natural* flavor of natural unprocessed Carolina Brand and River Brand Rice—and Mom is happy because cooking is so fast and simple.

TASTES BETTER NATURALLY!
COOKS QUICK NATURALLY!

A girl can't he

Fresh STICK DEODORANT
Checks Perspiration

EW CHIEFT

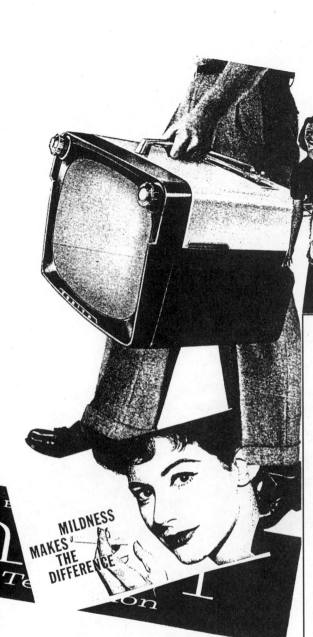

Midcentury America: What It Cost to Live

In 1950, the average American's salary was just under $3,000. That may not sound like much, but the money went a long way.

• Housing: Less than $500 paid the rent or mortgage for the whole year.

• Transportation: The family could buy a new Chevrolet for $1,329. A gallon of gas cost less than 30 cents.

• Food: A half-gallon of milk cost about 42 cents. A loaf of bread cost about 14 cents.

• Reading Material: The daily newspaper cost a nickel, and *Time* magazine was just 20 cents.

The government helped too. About 14 million Americans had entered the armed forces during World War II. They had interrupted their educations and their careers to serve their country. Now they were back in civilian life. To help them, Congress passed a law known as the G.I. Bill of Rights. (The initials *GI* meant "government issue." People called the infantrymen "GIs.") The G.I. Bill of Rights provided money for veterans to attend colleges and vocational schools. It also made low-interest loans available for GIs to buy houses and start businesses.

In addition, a baby boom took place between 1946 and 1960. For years, through the Great Depression and the war, couples had put off getting married and starting families. Those who had married tended to have small families. Now that the war was over, couples married earlier and had larger families. Between 1946 and 1960, America's population jumped by about 40 million. And all these new citizens needed goods and services.

Americans on a Spending Spree

Suppose your family's income in 1950 was $3,000. By 1960, it probably would have grown more than 57 percent, to $4,700. How did Americans spend their newfound wealth?

- Houses: In 1945, 20 million people owned their own home. By 1960, 33 million did. And most of the homes were new. Building them created jobs for bricklayers, carpenters, electricians, lumbermen, plumbers, and roofers, among other workers.
- Cars: The automobile industry boomed after the war. People who lived in the growing suburbs needed cars to travel to work. They also needed cars to shop, to drive children to school, and to visit the doctor and dentist. Many suburban families owned two cars. And more cars meant a boom in the businesses that helped them run – oil, glass, leather, metals, and rubber.
- Airplanes: The airplane industry boomed too. Many people could now afford to travel by air. That called not only for more planes but also for more runways and airports.

Factory workers assemble TV sets in 1950. These sets featured TV, AM/FM radio, and phonograph.

• Electronics: The new electronics industry grew quickly. Americans jumped from the age of radio into the age of television. In 1947, only a few people owned TV sets. By 1960, about 85 percent of American households had TVs.

• Stocks: Since the 1929 stock market crash, very few people had bought stocks. But from 1949 to 1950 alone, the total number of shares of stock traded on the New York Stock Exchange nearly doubled. By 1960, about 17 million Americans owned stocks. The money invested in American business helped it grow and prosper. ■

America's first jet airliner, the Boeing 707, first flew in 1958 on a Pan American transatlantic route.

THEN & NOW

For many Americans, owning a home has always been part of the American Dream. In 1949, a four-room house in Levittown, New York, sold for $7,990. If you added closing costs, landscaping, and kitchen appliances, the cost was about $10,000. There was a $90 down payment, and the mortgage was just $58 per month. By the mid-1950s, the average 30-year-old man could pay the mortgage on an average house with just 14 percent of his monthly paycheck — before taxes.

Today, the sons and daughters of that 1950s homeowner are spending 30 to 35 percent of their income — often two incomes per family — to pay the mortgage. Why? More people want houses, and the increased demand means higher prices. Also, houses today are larger, averaging six rooms rather than four. Many include such conveniences as dishwashers and air-conditioning, which raise the price. As more land has been developed for housing, fewer vacant lots are left. As a result, the cost of land has skyrocketed. Then, too, real estate taxes have soared as communities vote to spend more money for police, fire fighters, schools, and other services.

The Love Affair with the Car

High demand for cars keeps these 1950s autoworkers busy. Between 1946 and 1960, Americans bought 33 million new cars, like this Cadillac Sedan deVille (above).

Swooping fins. Glittering chrome. Long, low-slung bodies. Two-tone paint jobs. Hot rods. The cars of the 1950s were something to see!

Rolling Off the Assembly Line

Because of the war, carmakers stopped making cars from 1942 to 1945. Even after the war ended, steel and other goods needed to make cars were in short supply. But wartime ads had promised shiny new cars for returning soldiers. By 1946, automakers in Detroit were keeping their promise and rolling them out.

And Americans were buying them like never before. From 1930 to 1940, the number of cars in the United States had risen by only 3 million. Between 1946 and 1950, Americans bought 8 million new cars. They bought millions more during the 1950s. By 1960, there were 62 million cars on the road—one for every 1.8 adults.

The Open Road

Americans had their new cars. They also had a desire to travel. Now they needed better roads to drive on. Highways had not been kept in good shape during the war.

In 1956, President Eisenhower called for the biggest public-works project in history: construction of an interstate highway system. By the time it was finished, it covered 42,000 miles with four- and six-lane highways, and it cost $121 billion. Now, people could travel faster, farther, and more safely than ever before. Trucks could carry goods from state to state. By 1987, the interstate highway system, which made up just 1 percent of the nation's roads, was carrying 22 percent of the nation's motor traffic. ■

Carmakers have problems today that they did not have in the 1950s. One problem is competition from the Japanese. Union demands, antipollution and safety laws, and oil prices are other problems.

Do you think auto buyers should try to help with these problems? If so, how can they help?

Do you believe we should "buy American"—even if we think foreign cars are better bargains?

After the United States began building the interstate highway system in 1956, the "cloverleaf" intersection started to become a common sight.

THEN & NOW

In 1960, most Americans bought cars that were built by one of the "big three" automakers—General Motors, Ford, and Chrysler. In 1990, four of the 10 top-selling cars in the United States were Japanese: the Honda Accord, the Toyota Camry, the Honda Civic, and the Toyota Corolla. Japanese manufacturers held almost 25 percent of the U.S. car market.

Many people believe that Japanese automakers will take over more and more of the American car market. Their cars look good. They are well built and are improved often. Also, the Japanese have recently started making car models they have not produced before. For example, in November 1990, a new station wagon arrived in Honda showrooms. Soon after, Honda introduced a slick sports car with a price tag of $64,000. With much fanfare, Japan has entered the luxury car market. Toyota developed a minivan and is thinking about building a big pickup truck. By 1995, one out of three cars in the United States may carry a Japanese nameplate.

A Stormy Time for Unions

Steelworkers preparing for a strike in 1949. Many strikes occurred during the postwar years.

America's workers, who had suffered so much during the Great Depression of the 1930s, benefited a great deal from World War II. The war had helped end the Depression in the United States. For the first time since the late 1920s, almost everyone who wanted to work had a job. What's more, many worked overtime. For each hour of overtime, they typically received 1½ times their usual pay. As a result, workers were, in general, earning more money. Between 1941 and 1945, average weekly earnings grew from $24.20 to $44.39.

At the same time, workers contributed a great deal to the wartime production miracle. Never before had U.S. factories turned out so many goods. In addition to working hard, people worked steadily. They agreed not to strike as long as the war lasted.

Postwar Inflation

During the war, the government had tried to keep a lid on prices. Landlords were not allowed to raise rents. Wages and salaries were frozen – kept at the same level. Corporations had to pay a special tax on excess profits. And gasoline, shoes, coffee, and other goods were rationed. You could buy them only if you had money *and* a ration coupon. Nevertheless, the cost of living rose about 30 percent between 1939 and 1945.

Once the war ended, it was no longer possible to keep the lid on. Rationing ended, and price controls were gradually lifted. After the war, everyone wanted to buy things they'd been without. They were eager to pay for them—whatever the price. As a result, *inflation* (a rise in prices) immediately became a serious problem. By August of 1946, the cost of living had risen 75 percent. As a headline in the *New York Daily News* put it: PRICES SOAR, BUYERS SORE.

A Wave of Strikes

One result of the postwar inflation was many more labor strikes. For almost two years, it seemed that every time people opened a newspaper, they read about another strike. The strikes were usually for higher wages. Workers wanted their income to keep up with inflation.

In 1946 alone, more than 4.6 million workers went out on nearly 5,000 strikes. First the steelworkers went out—for 80 days. That kept other industries that used steel—such as carmakers—from producing goods. As soon as the steelworkers returned to the job, the coal miners went out. In those years, coal supplied 62 percent of the nation's electricity and 55 percent of its industrial power. Soon, cities around the country were cutting the use of electricity during certain hours. Railroads cut the number of trains they ran. Industrial plants shut down.

The unions won large pay hikes. They also won such "fringe benefits" as paid vacations, paid holidays, health insurance, and retirement plans. Some unions won cost-of-living allowances. That meant that if the cost of living went up, wages would go up too.

Rising Tensions

President Truman usually supported labor unions. He thought that workers had the right to bargain for higher wages and better working conditions. But he was against strikes that hurt the nation as a whole. So he used his powers to end certain strikes. For example, he ended a railroad strike by threatening to draft the strikers into the army.

President Truman was not the only person getting angry about the actions of labor unions. Many Americans began to think that the unions were too powerful. They were afraid that the long strikes would hurt the new prosperity in the country. They called union leaders "strike-happy." They also began to fear that the unions were run by Communists.

The Taft-Hartley Act

In 1947, Congress decided that the time had come to control organized labor. So it passed the Labor-Management Relations Act of 1947, better known as the Taft-Hartley Act.

These union members thought the Taft-Hartley Act went too far. President Truman agreed and vetoed the bill. But Congress passed the law over his veto.

What did the new law do? It said that workers did not have to belong to a union to get a job. It also said that workers did not have to join a union after they were hired. The law also set "cooling-off periods" before strikes. That meant the president could make unions wait 80 days before they went on strike. In addition, to keep unions from influencing government leaders, the Taft-Hartley Act said that unions could not give money to political campaigns. Union leaders also had to sign an oath that they were not Communists.

President Truman felt the Taft-Hartley Act went too far. In his opinion, it was "a clear threat to the successful working of our democratic society." So he *vetoed*, or rejected, it. But Congress passed the law over the president's veto. Congress can "override" a presidential veto if two-thirds of the members of both houses vote to do so.

Labor Regroups

The two most important union leaders after World War II were George Meany and Walter Reuther. Meany was elected president of the American Federation of Labor (AFL) in 1952. The AFL was an organization of craft unions whose members were all skilled workers, such as carpenters or welders. Reuther became the head of the United Automobile Workers (UAW) in 1946. His union belonged to the Congress of Industrial Organizations (CIO). The CIO organized workers by industry, such as autoworkers and steelworkers. CIO unions included unskilled as well as skilled workers.

The AFL and the CIO differed in other ways besides how they were organized. For instance, the AFL was strongly anti-Communist. The CIO had Communists among its members. But in 1949, the CIO threw out several unions because their leaders were Communists or agreed with Communist ideas. That made it possible for the two groups to strengthen their position by merging into a single organization.

Reuther became the head of the CIO in 1952. He led the fight to merge the two labor organizations. In 1955, they became the AFL-CIO, with a membership of 15 million workers. Meany became the new group's first president. Reuther became its first vice president. ■

During the 1950s, many people thought that unions had "gone too far." Many people think so now too.

Do you think unions are too "strike-happy"?

Do you think wages for union members have gotten too high?

Do you think workers who are needed for public safety—fire fighters, police—should be allowed to strike?

Despite Taft-Hartley, unions can still give money to candidates through PACs— political action committees. Should these committees be against the law?

George Meany (left) of the American Federation of Labor and Walter Reuther (right) of the Congress of Industrial Organizations celebrating the merger of the two labor organizations.

The Common Market

In 1962, Galeries Lafayette, a leading department store in Paris, France, set up an eye-opening display of goods. Each item on display had two price tags: the first from 1958, the second from 1962. For example:

• A camera from West Germany: $87.00 vs. $50.30.
• A raincoat from Italy: $22.00 vs. $8.00.
• A French-made refrigerator: $166.00 vs. $101.00.

Why two price tags? To show the price changes the Common Market had brought about in just three years.

Before World War II, it was hard for the countries of Europe to trade with one another. Each country placed tariffs, or high import taxes, on goods from other countries. They often refused to sell goods to their neighbors.

After World War II, European countries needed to rebuild their economies. They also wanted to prevent another war.

Jean Monnet, a French banker and public official, came up with an idea. Why not organize European trade the same way the United States was organized? In the United States, goods and people move easily between states. Why couldn't goods and people move easily between the nations of Europe? The United States had a home market of 180 million consumers. European nations had only 10 to 50 million consumers *each.* If the European countries could trade with each other, they could sell to many more consumers.

In 1950, Monnet made the first step toward a common European market. He convinced the French foreign

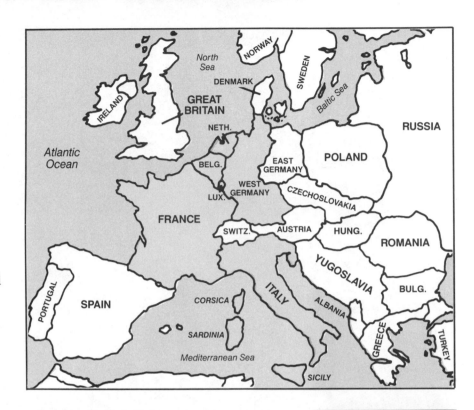

minister, Robert Schuman, to suggest that France and Germany pool their coal and steel resources. Instead of each nation controlling some of the coal fields and iron mines of the Rhine River basin, the two nations would operate the coal fields and iron mines together. That would allow them to get rid of some facilities and to lower prices. Steel production would rise. So would wages and profits.

On March 25, 1957, France, West Germany, Belgium, Italy, Luxembourg, and the Netherlands signed the Treaty of Rome. The treaty created the European Economic Community (EEC), usually called the Common Market. Under the Common Market, there would be no tariffs on all goods traded among the six countries. The six countries also agreed to try to pass similar laws about farm prices, taxes, transportation, and welfare. ■

In 1957, the European Economic Community, or Common Market, was formed. The map shows the EEC nations in gray.

Judgment at Nuremberg

Nazi leaders listening to the charges against them at the Nuremberg trials. The court found 19 of the 22 Nazis guilty of war crimes.

They didn't look like monsters. They sat up straight behind long tables, well dressed and neatly groomed. They looked ahead calmly. They might have been professors listening to a lecture. But they weren't. They were men on trial, most of them for their lives. They were accused of some of the worst crimes in the history of the world, crimes that cost millions of lives.

The time: November 1945. The place: Nuremberg, Germany. The event: the Nuremberg trials, in which 22 Nazi leaders faced justice for their evil crimes. The trials would last more than 10 months.

The Nazi leaders were being tried by an International Military Tribunal (court). On the court were eight judges from Great Britain, France, the United

States, and the Soviet Union. These judges would decide the fate of the Nuremberg 22.

There was a new idea behind the trial. In the past, government leaders had not been brought to trial for war crimes. But after World War II, things changed. The tribunal said that leaders who had broken international laws *could* be put on trial. And there was strong evidence that Nazis had broken many international laws.

Four Charges Against the Nazis

The defendants—the Nazi leaders—were charged with four crimes. The first: planning to commit crimes. The court thought that planning crimes was a crime in itself.

The second charge was "crimes against peace." This referred to making war against peaceful countries. Evidence was easy to find; Germany had invaded countries throughout Europe.

"War crimes" was the third charge. Even war has its rules, and the court accused the Nazis of breaking these rules. Evidence of Nazi war crimes was

the Germans' cruel treatment of Soviet prisoners of war. The Soviet prisoners were often tortured, murdered, or used in cruel medical experiments. Many were killed slowly by being starved or left out in the cold.

The fourth charge was "crimes against humanity." The tribunal defined these crimes as "murder, extermination, enslavement, deportation, and other inhumane acts committed against any civilian population, before or during the war. . . ." The Allies found plenty of evidence of Nazi crimes against humanity. When the Germans invaded a country, they took whatever they wanted. That included people. Nazis often shipped them to Germany as slave labor. The Nazis also sent people to concentration camps, where millions were killed. Six million European Jews alone were put to death in these camps. This was Nazi leader Adolf Hitler's "final solution" to what he called the "Jewish problem."

A picture, as they say, is worth a thousand words: this little Warsaw boy was one victim of Nazi "crimes against humanity."

"Crimes against humanity" was a key concept at Nuremberg. Under this concept, some actions are so bad that they are an insult to all human beings. And the court accused the Nazis of committing these crimes.

For months, the Nuremberg 22 defended themselves. Few admitted any guilt. Many said they had simply followed orders. However, the court found 19 of the defendants guilty. Seven went to jail—three of them for life. The remaining 12 were given the death sentence. ∎

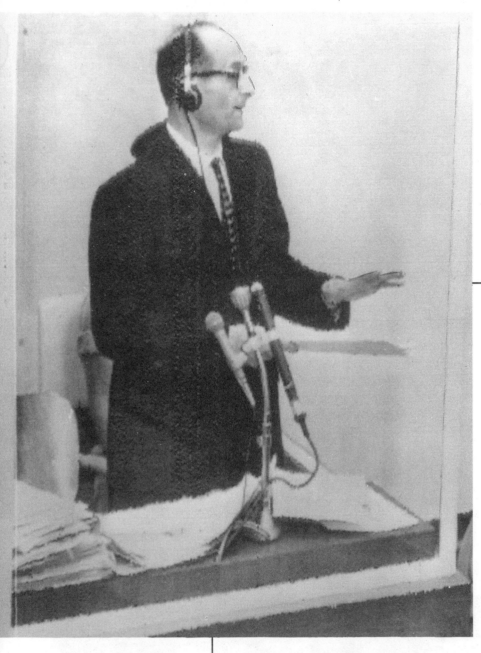

Nazi Adolf Eichmann testifying from a bullet-proof glass booth in 1961. He was found guilty and was hanged.

Adolf Eichmann: In the Glass Booth

Nazi Adolf Eichmann escaped the Nuremberg trials. But he didn't escape the government of Israel, which searched for him for years. Eichmann had been in charge of sending European Jews to the concentration camps. He had sent millions to their death.

In 1960, Israeli agents found Eichmann in Argentina. They kidnapped him and smuggled him back to Israel for trial. At the trial, many people heard the details about the Holocaust for the first time.

Israel was very careful with its prisoner. Eichmann was watched constantly. He slept in a bomb-proof cell and appeared in court in a bullet-proof glass booth.

Like most of the Nuremberg 22, Eichmann admitted no guilt. He was just an officer who had followed orders, he said. But the evidence said something else. It showed that he loved his terrible work. People were shocked to hear, for example, that Eichmann had once sent 4,000 children to the Auschwitz death camp.

He was found guilty on December 11, 1961. Eichmann angrily refused to accept the verdict. "I am not the monster I am made out to be," he insisted. His appeal was rejected, and Eichmann was hanged on May 31, 1962.

The McCarthy Era

Politicians and private citizens were afraid of McCarthy — he could ruin their reputations in one sentence.

"**A**re you now or have you ever been a Communist?"

This was a question many Americans feared in the early 1950s. America was a nation living in fear. Americans feared Communists – and they feared being *called* Communists.

Some people used this fear to help their careers. Most successful at this was U.S. Senator Joseph R. McCarthy from Wisconsin. Because of him, the early 1950s are often called the McCarthy Era.

How the Fear Began

Fear of Communists did not begin with McCarthy. The U.S. Congress began to worry about Communists in the late 1930s. Congressman Martin Dies thought that some members of the government were Communists. In 1938, Dies helped form a special House Un-American Activities Committee (HUAC). Its purpose was to find Communists and other "un-American" people across the nation.

HUAC would hound Americans well into the 1960s. It ran on "guilt by association": if you knew people who were under suspicion, you were under suspicion too. HUAC didn't care how weak the evidence was. It didn't care who gave the evidence. It spread rumors about people who were under suspicion. These rumors ruined the lives of many innocent people.

During World War II, Americans and Soviet Communists were allies. The Nazis were their common enemy. After the war, however, the Communists set up governments in the countries of Eastern Europe. Anti-Communist feelings grew strong again in the United States. In 1947, President Harry S. Truman created the federal employee loyalty program. Under this program, people could lose their jobs – not for anything they'd done, but for how they thought and who they knew. Americans' fear of communism seemed to be spreading.

ROSENBERGS EXECUTED AS ATOM SPIES AFTER SUPREME COURT VACATES STAY; LAST-MINUTE PLEA TO PRESIDENT FAILS

Their Death Penalty Carried Out   PAIR SILENT TO END

Julius and Ethel Rosenberg are taken from court in a U.S. marshal's van after being convicted of spying. Both were later executed.

government. For them, that would explain the mess the world was in.

McCarthy began making dramatic speeches in the Senate. He used *slander*—lies to hurt someone's reputation—in these speeches. But by law, slander was not illegal on the Senate floor. McCarthy publicly accused people who were both in and out of the government. Another senator criticized him for doing this. McCarthy acted outraged. "Crocodile tears are being shed here for traitorous individuals . . . ," he said. He then implied that traitors in the U.S. State Department had helped Communists gain control of China. People believed this slander. Those watching the debate in the Senate applauded.

The Rosenbergs and the McCarran Act

Political events of 1950 added to Americans' fear of Communists.

That summer, married couple Julius and Ethel Rosenberg were accused of being Communist spies. The charge? Giving secrets about the atomic bomb to the Soviets during World War II. Today, the case against the Rosenbergs seems weak. It was based on the testimony of Ethel Rosenberg's brother, who testified against her to get a lighter sentence himself. The Rosenbergs *were* "lefties"—believers in communism— but many people did not believe they were spies. Others did not want the Rosenbergs to die for their crime. After a very public trial, the Rosenbergs were convicted of treason—betraying their country. Despite protests all over the world, they were put to death in 1953. They are the only non-military Americans ever executed for spying.

Senator McCarthy Swoops Down

Wisconsin's senator Joseph R. McCarthy smelled the fear—and made the most of it. McCarthy, who began his first term in the Senate in 1947, had done little in his time in office. He had not written any important laws. Other senators thought he was a fool. McCarthy needed a hot issue to help his career. Communism was it.

McCarthy made his move on February 9, 1950. He announced that he had a list of 205 Communists still working for the State Department. McCarthy had no list. He was making it up as he went along. Yet people began to believe McCarthy. Some people wanted to believe that Communists had taken over our

The U.S. Congress shared and added to Americans' fear of communism. In 1950, Congress passed the McCarran Internal Security Act. This act required all U.S. Communists to register on a list. It also set up detention camps to imprison traitors in an emergency. No one was ever put into these prisons, but knowing that the camps existed was enough to worry many. Fear of communism seemed out of control.

McCarthy Unleashes His Dogs

Republicans won by a landslide in the 1952 elections. For the first time in 20 years, America had a Republican president. Senator McCarthy, whose career had seemed troubled until he discovered communism, was reelected as well.

McCarthy became chairman of the Permanent Subcommittee on Investigations in the Senate in 1953. Using this committee, he attacked dozens of people and organizations. Politicians and private citizens were afraid of him—he could ruin their reputations in one sentence. *McCarthyism* became the term used to describe the ways he slandered and frightened people.

Television Exposes McCarthy

Respected newsman Edward R. Murrow helped America see the danger of McCarthyism.

During World War II, Murrow had often risked his life to cover the battles. Now, he risked his career as a TV newscaster. In late 1953, Murrow's show "See It Now" looked into McCarthyism. It told the story of U.S. Air Force lieutenant Milo Radulovich. The lieutenant had been discharged by the air force. Why? Because he refused to have nothing to do with his sister and father. They were thought to have

Radio and TV newscaster Edward R. Murrow risked his career to criticize Senator Joseph McCarthy.

pro-Communist ideas, though even this was not certain. After Murrow's program, the air force let Radulovich back in.

On March 19, 1954, "See It Now" focused on McCarthy himself. It showed films and played tapes of his speeches. Viewers took a good look, and many didn't like what they saw. Public opinion began to turn against McCarthy.

McCarthy vs. the Army

When McCarthy took on the United States Army, he lost even more public support. McCarthy began feuding with the army early in 1954.

First, he accused an army general of protecting Communists in the army. He rudely insulted the general. That upset the army. Second, one of McCarthy's aides, G. David Schine, had been drafted in 1953. McCarthy's team had tried to "pull strings" so that Schine could have an easy ride in the army. Finally, the army exposed the McCarthy team's actions in the *New York Times*. In return, McCarthy accused the army of keeping Schine so that Schine could not expose army Communists. The Senate held hearings

FRIDAY, DECEMBER 3, 1954.

FINAL VOTE CONDEMNS M'CARTHY, 67-22, FOR ABUSING SENATE AND COMMITTEE; ZWICKER COUNT ELIMINATED IN DEBATE

R WARNS
GHT WING;
KNOWLAND

ty Must Follow
sive Course or
oss of Influence

t and summary of the
conference, Page 18.

WILLIAM S. WHITE

RANCOR CONTINUES

Welker Refuses to Let
Flanders Apology Go
Record

REPUBLICANS SPLIT

Democrats Act Solidly
in Support of Motion
Against Senator

COMMUNIST PARTY ORGANIZATION U.S.A-FEB. 9, 1950

McCarthy (standing) testifying at the army-McCarthy hearings. The army's lawyer, Joseph Welch (sitting at table), asked him "Have you no sense of decency . . . ?"

to sort out all of the accusations. The hearings were on TV. They showed more than 20 million viewers just how brutal and unfair McCarthy was. His dishonesty became clear to the nation. TV viewers saw that he would attack and slander people at the drop of a hat – and would pay little attention to the facts.

In an unforgettable moment, the army's lawyer, Joseph N. Welch, asked McCarthy, "Have you no sense of decency. . . ?" This scolding by the fatherly, well-respected Welch hit home with viewers. It may have led to McCarthy's downfall more than anything else.

McCarthy had lost his greatest weapon: fear. People no longer took him seriously, so they no longer feared him. Now the Senate felt safe in condemning McCarthy. They censured – officially disapproved of – him in December of 1954. He had been guilty of "conduct unbecoming a Senator." Most Americans still did not like Communists. But by the mid-1950s, calling someone a Communist could no longer ruin a person's life. The McCarthy Era was over. ■

The House Un-American Activities Committee no longer exists. Do you think such a committee is needed? What is an "un-American" activity? Who should decide what this means? Should people be punished for their political beliefs?

A Battle Between Church and State

"**C**ongress shall make no law respecting an establishment of religion. . . ." So begins the First Amendment to our Constitution. The amendment says that our government should have no religious ties—that *church* and *state* should be separate. This separation, however, has often meant different things to different people.

How It Happened

Before 1948, public schools offered "released-time" programs. People from different churches could teach religion on school grounds once a week. Students who had been "released" by their parents could attend these free classes. Students who did not attend

10-year-old James once had to spend the period sitting in the hall.

McCollum sued the school board of Champaign, Illinois. She asked that they stop the released-time program. Her lawyer said it went against the First Amendment to the U.S. Constitution. The local court disagreed. McCollum took her case to the Illinois Supreme Court. This court also disagreed with her lawyer. So she went all the way to the U.S. Supreme Court. On March 8, 1948, its judges agreed with her.

Was It Unconstitutional?

Justice Hugo L. Black said that the use of tax-supported public schools for religious teachings clearly went against the First Amendment. The court's decision didn't settle everything. Only the program in Champaign, Illinois, was declared unconstitutional—against the law. Other programs might still be OK. However, schools did not want to risk lawsuits. Many schools threw out all programs that had anything to do with religion. ∎

Vashti McCollum and her son. McCollum's lawsuit led to the end of "released-time" religious programs in public schools.

could use the period for schoolwork. By 1948, some 2,200 communities offered released-time programs. Vashti McCollum, whose son attended public school, protested. She didn't believe in God, and she did not want her son to attend the classes. He was the only student who did not attend. His classmates teased him. McCollum said

THEN & NOW

Politicians continue to struggle with the question of religion in the schools today. In the 1980s, President Ronald Reagan wanted the Senate to pass a "prayer amendment." It would have allowed students to say prayers in school if they wanted to. Reagan's amendment was voted down after a two-week Senate debate. But moments of silence and other forms of prayer are still being used—and challenged. Will this controversy ever end?

School Desegregation: The Great Step

It's always hard being the new kid in school. But imagine being the new kid *and* having to face an ugly mob each day—a mob that doesn't want you there. And imagine needing armed guards to protect you from the mob. Back in 1957, nine students went to high school under these conditions. The reason? They were the first black students to attend a whites-only Arkansas school. And they weren't welcome.

Separate but Unequal

Why weren't blacks and whites going to the same schools all along? Segregation had kept them apart. Segregation is the separation of races— in this case, of blacks and whites. Segregation existed across the United States, but it was the *law* in the Deep South. A Supreme Court ruling in 1896 had upheld segregation. The court had ruled that segregation was lawful as long as whites and blacks had equal *accommodations*, or buildings and services.

There was a problem with this "separate but equal" idea, however. Black schools were never equal to those for whites—not even close. Many black schools were little more than one-room shacks.

First Steps to Equality

Supported by the National Association for the Advancement of Colored People (NAACP), black lawyers began to challenge the "separate but equal" idea in the 1930s.

Colleges were their first target. Charles Hamilton Houston and his star law student, Thurgood Marshall (later a Supreme Court justice), filed lawsuits for discrimination against the Universities of Maryland and Missouri. They won both cases. Both schools were told to let African-American students attend. This victory began a series of court challenges.

Brown v. Board of Education of Topeka was the biggest court challenge. This famous lawsuit ended segregation in U.S. public schools. The case went before the Supreme Court in December 1952. The court took more than a year to make a decision. Finally, on May 17, 1954, the court ruled that segregation

In 1954, the Supreme Court ruled that school segregation was against the law. This led to scenes like the one below.

was illegal: "We conclude, that in the field of public education . . .'separate but equal' has no place. Separate educational facilities are inherently unequal," the court said. The South prepared to fight.

The Little Rock Crisis

For the first time, black students had the law behind them. But who would enforce it, and when? The court had not said *when* segregation had to end. Southern states moved slowly, if at all. Three years passed without any change. The NAACP sued the state of Arkansas to make it move faster.

Arkansas planned to start by desegregating one school, Little Rock Central High School. The school board accepted nine black students out of 75 applicants. But that was nine too many for Arkansas governor Orval Faubus.

Protesters shouting at student Elizabeth Eckford as she enters Little Rock Central High School in 1957.

NAACP lawyer Thurgood Marshall (center) sitting on the steps of the Supreme Court with some of the students who broke the color barrier at Little Rock Central High School. Years later, Marshall became the first black Supreme Court justice.

On the first day of school in 1957, he ordered the National Guard to surround Central High. He said they were there to prevent rioting. But they were really there to keep the black students from entering the school.

Weeks later, Governor Faubus finally removed his troops. On September 23, the students finally got into school— through a side entrance, escorted by police. But an angry mob gathered outside. By noon, it was clear the police were outnumbered. They could not control the situation. They rounded up the nine students and tried to decide what to do. Finally, they escorted the students through the mob and drove them home.

Sending in the Troops

The mob was too unruly for the local police to control, however. Little Rock's mayor was forced to seek help from the U.S. government. By the next evening, President Eisenhower had sent it. Troops arrived in jeeps; the mobs disappeared. By late September, things were calmer. The National Guard stayed at Central High throughout the rest of the school year.

Governor Faubus was not through. In 1958, he decided to close all of Little Rock's schools completely. If he couldn't stop integration, he figured, he'd stop the schools. This move was illegal. He could not enforce it. Almost a year later, by order of a court, schools reopened. Little Rock's public schools were integrated at last. ∎

A Tough First Day of School

Melba Pattillo Beals never forgot her first day at Central High. She was one of the Little Rock Nine— the first blacks to attend Central High. She recalls that "even the adults, the school officials, were panicked. A couple of the black kids who were with me were crying. Someone made a suggestion that if they allowed the mob to hang one kid, then they could get the rest out. . . ." Luckily, the police chief stopped that kind of talk. He loaded the nine students into two cars. The drivers were told to keep going, no matter what. Beals's driver got students through the mob and safely home. ". . . and I remember saying, 'Thank you for the ride.' I should have said, 'Thank you for my life,'" Beals added.

The Civil Rights Movement

FOR COLORED ONLY

Segregation was the law in the South for many years.

To live where you like. To drink from a public water fountain. To eat at a lunch counter. To vote. In the mid-1950s, blacks began to organize for these and other basic rights. What caused the civil rights movement to pick up speed? As much as any other single event, it was the murder of Emmett Till.

Emmett Till Meets Racism

Till was a 14-year-old from Chicago. He had relatives in Mississippi. He visited them in August 1955. While there, he is said to have talked "fresh" to a white woman: he called to her, "Bye, baby." Days later, the woman's husband and his half-brother kidnapped the boy. Within a week,

fth ... of the se.
as the number Stengel had
redicted last April would be | Continued on Page 13, Column 1

Mississippi Jury Acquits 2 Accused in Youth's Killing

By JOHN N. POPHAM

Special to The New York Times.

SUMNER, Miss., Sept. 23—Two Missi
accused of the murder of Emmett Louis
Chicago Negro, were acquitted today. A ju
neighbors of the defendants
reached the verdict after one
hour and five minutes of de-
liberations.

Roy Bryant, 24-year-old country store keeper, and his half-
brother, J. W. Milam, 36, both
born and reared in Tallahatchie
County, where the trial was held,
greeted the verdict by embrac-
w...

Till's body turned up in the Tallahatchie River. He had been beaten so badly that his relatives could identify him only by a ring.

The Till case was talked about across the country. It gave the public a look at the deadly results of racism. The trial of the boy's killers showed Americans what southern justice could be like. Till's murderers were found not guilty. Throughout the United States, people were outraged. More than ever, many blacks felt it was time to demand their rights.

The Montgomery Bus Boycott

A few months after Till's death, black leaders found a battle to fight. In Montgomery, Alabama, blacks were

abused by the city's bus system. Blacks paid the same bus fare as whites. But after paying it, blacks had to leave the bus and reenter it through the back door. Blacks had to sit in the back. If the bus got crowded, they had to give up their seats to whites.

Rosa Parks, a black seamstress, was tired of this treatment. In December 1955, she refused to give up her seat to a white man. The driver had her arrested.

The African-American community supported her. They organized a bus boycott. A *boycott* — a refusal to buy a

Emmett Till, who was brutally murdered in Mississippi — and the all-white jury that freed his killers.

Rosa Parks was arrested in 1955 for refusing to give up her bus seat to a white man. Here, she is sitting in the front of the bus after the Supreme Court banned bus segregation one year later.

product or use a service – puts pressure on a company or an organization to change its ways. The blacks in Montgomery wanted the bus company to change its ways of treating blacks. A one-day boycott was so successful that black leaders decided to continue it. They formed the Montgomery Improvement Association (MIA) to help keep the boycott going. And Reverend Martin Luther King, Jr., was chosen as their leader. The MIA would try to talk with city leaders and the bus company about changing the rules.

The other side angrily refused to negotiate. So black bus riders stayed away. They got to work any way they could; they formed car pools, rode bicycles, or walked. Months went by. Tension grew. Several homes were bombed, including King's. The leaders of the boycott were arrested. But King's arrest backfired. Suddenly, national attention focused on him and the situation in Montgomery. In November 1956, the Supreme Court ruled that bus segregation was unconstitutional. The next month, buses finally were integrated. It was the first clear victory for the civil rights movement.

Black southern churches had supported the Montgomery boycott.

They formed an organization called the Southern Christian Leadership Conference (SCLC) to continue the civil rights struggle. The SCLC elected King as its president. King's leadership would play a big part in the coming fights for freedom. ■

The Montgomery bus boycott was the first time southern blacks demonstrated their economic strength. By hurting the bus company's business, they brought about change. Do you think a boycott is a good way of changing things that are unfair? What present-day injustices do you think a boycott might be used against?

Rev. Dr. Martin Luther King, Jr.: Freedom's Voice

When he agreed to head the Montgomery Improvement Association in 1955, little did Martin Luther King, Jr., know that he would soon become the spokesman for the civil rights movement. He said he had no talent for organization. But King did have a sharp sense of timing, of knowing when to make a move. Best of all, he had a way of speaking that could move even the hardest heart. Not everyone liked what he said. But when he spoke, the nation listened. King spoke for a people who were tired of being put down and denied basic freedoms. By protesting nonviolently, they would meet "physical force with soul force," as King said. To those who were unfair to blacks, King said, "Do to us what you will and we will still love you. We cannot in all good conscience obey your unjust laws." King often went to jail for his beliefs. He was killed on April 4, 1968, by a man filled with hate. But King's message of love and understanding lives on.

Rev. Martin Luther King, Jr., and his wife Coretta leave the Montgomery (Alabama) Court House in 1956. King was arrested for organizing the Montgomery bus boycott.

Living in the Nuclear Age

FEBRUARY 1, 1950.

FIVE CENTS

TRUMAN ORDERS HYDROGEN BOMB BUILT FOR SECURITY PENDING AN ATOMIC PACT; HAILS STEP; BOARD BEGINS JOB

HISTORIC DECISION

The U.S. testing an atomic bomb at Bikini Atoll in 1946.

In August 1945, the United States dropped atomic bombs on two Japanese cities. The bombs ended World War II. They also frightened the nations of the world. The United States was the only nation that had an atom bomb, and other nations thought we had many of them.

The United States had a little secret, though: it had no more atomic bombs. "There was not a single operable atomic bomb in the 'vault,'" recalled David Lilienthal, head of the U.S. Atomic Energy Commission.

In the late 1940s, the United States raced to rebuild its stockpile of atomic weapons. The Soviet Union also worked to build an A-bomb, successfully exploding one in 1949. The race was on. American and Soviet scientists raced to build the most powerful atomic weapons. Within a few years, both countries would have enough atomic weapons to destroy the world many times over.

On January 31, 1950, President Truman decided to build another bomb as well. The hydrogen bomb, or H-bomb, was many times more powerful than existing A-bombs. The H-bomb was the start of a new, more deadly part of the nuclear arms race.

Ashes of Death

The United States exploded its first H-bomb in November 1952. Nine months later, the Soviets also exploded an H-bomb. The two superpowers tested bigger, more powerful nuclear weapons throughout the mid-1950s. But scientists soon discovered troubling effects from these tests.

Nuclear bombs create tremendous heat and pressure when they explode. They also give off a deadly, invisible form of energy called *radioactivity*. An exploding nuclear bomb throws huge amounts of radioactive dust and dirt miles into the air. Scientists called this radioactive material *fallout,* because it "falls out" of the sky.

Winds can carry fallout from a nuclear test hundreds of miles away.

Nuclear Fears

Families racing into their basements, trying to see how fast they could get there. Public buildings with big, blue-and-yellow "fallout shelter" signs. Schoolchildren practicing "duck and cover" in front of their lockers in school hallways. These were common sights in the United States in the late 1950s. Americans were practicing what they would do if "the big one" were to land on their city.

Nuclear fears became part of American life. Popular science fiction movies imagined the effects of nuclear radiation on animals. For instance, in one movie, desert lizards were caught in nuclear tests. They grew to the size of dinosaurs and terrorized cities! Books such as Nevil Shute's *On the Beach* explored people's reactions after a nuclear explosion.

Because people were afraid of nuclear war, local and national governments made plans to protect people during a nuclear attack. Many public buildings served as fallout shelters. These shelters would—supposedly—protect people from fallout and from the blast of an atomic bomb explosion. Some people dug fallout shelters in their backyards. Children huddled in school gyms and basements to practice what to do in a nuclear attack.

The radiation from the fallout causes sickness and death in humans and animals. A Japanese fishing boat was once covered by fallout from a South Pacific bomb test. The fishermen, many of whom became ill, called the fallout "the ashes of death."

Many U.S. nuclear bombs were tested at Bikini Atoll, an island in the South Pacific. By the mid-1950s, the island and nearby water were very radioactive. People who tried to live there became sick from the radiation. A 1978 test proved that radiation levels in the area were still not safe for humans.

The United States and the Soviet

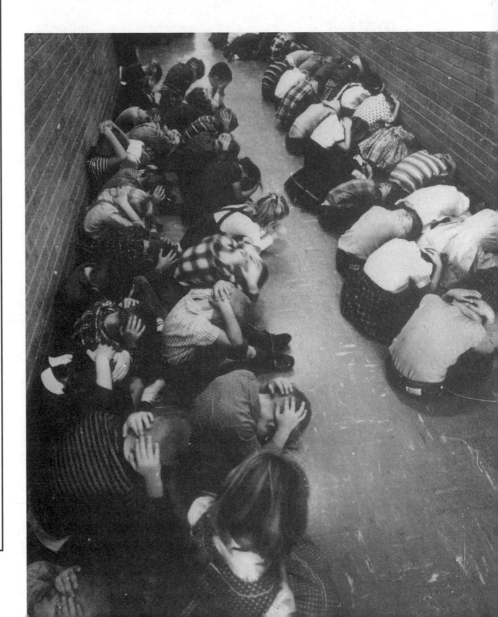

Kansas schoolchildren practicing for nuclear war survival in a 1960 civil defense drill.

> **A Japanese fishing boat was once covered by fallout from a South Pacific bomb test. The fishermen, many of whom became ill, called the fallout "the ashes of death."**

Union worried about radioactivity. Both sides knew they already had enough atomic weapons to completely destroy the Earth. So they agreed to stop nuclear testing in 1958. The test ban would last for three years.

The Peaceful Atom

Scientists did more with atomic energy than make bombs. They also looked for peaceful ways to use it. Nuclear power is one way they found.

Bombs are uncontrolled nuclear reactions. When a bomb explodes, all the energy is released in an instant. But by controlling the nuclear reaction, scientists can release the energy slowly, bit by bit. This energy can be used to heat water and make steam. The steam then runs electrical generators and makes electricity.

After 1954, a law allowed companies and other private groups to own and run atomic reactors. (The U.S. government checks the reactors to

make sure they are being run safely.) By the end of the 1950s, several nuclear reactors were generating electricity. ■

Should the United States use nuclear power to make electricity? Americans disagree. Some say it's the cheapest—and safest—way to provide energy. Others say the possibility of a nuclear accident is real and that all nuclear power plants should close. What do you say? To help you decide, you might write to the following two groups for information:

Here is a group that supports nuclear energy: American Nuclear Society
555 N. Kensington Ave.
LaGrange Park, IL 60525

Here is a group that opposes "nukes":
Nuclear Information and Resource Service
1424 16th St., N.W., #601
Washington, DC 20036

THEN & NOW

In the 1950s, fear of nuclear war caused antinuclear movements to grow rapidly. These groups worried most about nuclear weapons. In Britain and Europe, the Campaign for Nuclear Disarmament (CND) was an important antinuclear group. In the United States, many "Ban the Bomb" groups protested in the streets. All these groups wanted governments to stop making new nuclear weapons. They also wanted existing nuclear weapons to be destroyed.

Today's nuclear protesters— sometimes called no-nukes groups—are more worried about nuclear power plants. Massive accidents at nuclear power plants—Pennsylvania's Three Mile Island in 1979 and the Soviet Union's Chernobyl in 1986— released deadly radioactivity. Many people came to believe nuclear power plants were a greater threat than nuclear weapons. In 1980, David Lilienthal had this to say: "Bombs we now have, by the thousands . . . but we do not yet have a safe method of producing atomic electricity. This is the hard fact that America must face."

Speeding Up Communication

Faster! Faster! Everything in the 1950s seemed to move faster than in earlier years. And one of the fastest changes of all came in the way Americans communicate. Radios, telephones, and computers all saw changes in the 1950s – changes that led to swifter, cheaper communication.

The Transistor Takes Over

Every teenager in the late 1950s, it seemed, had a transistor radio glued to the ear. Transistor radios first came on the market in the late 1950s. They were lightweight and very convenient. They could run on batteries. Because they were small, they were easy to carry. This changed the listening habits of the entire nation.

The *transistor* – a device to control electrical flow – was the invention that made these radios possible. Three scientists working at Bell Labs in New Jersey announced the invention in 1948. It took nearly 10 years for the transistor to be manufactured. But then, it became a part of American life.

"Operator. May I Help You?"

Telephone conversations around the world became clearer and easier in the 1950s. Scientists improved telephone technology so that calls had less static. In addition, telephone companies laid more and more transoceanic cables, making it easier than ever to talk to the rest of the world.

Copy, Copy

Today, we depend on it for communications, but 40 years ago no one even knew there was a need for it. What is "it"? The photocopier.

American scientist Chester Carlson invented the process of *xerography* (dry writing) in 1938. It took more than 20 years to make an easy-to-use photocopying machine for the public. But in 1959, with the production of the first Xerox 914, the era of the copier was born.

Transistors (above left) allowed electric devices, such as radios and computers, to become much smaller. This ad (below) for transistor radios ran in 1957.

Fits in your purse for music *Wherever you go!*

WESTINGHOUSE

Inventor Chester Carlson (right) with the original Xerox copier. The first computer (left) was the 30-ton ENIAC, built in 1946.

Electronic Brains

The first computer – built in 1946 – was huge. It was almost two stories high, weighed 30 tons, and needed as much space as a railway boxcar. It had hundreds of switches, long and twisting cables, and a big fan on top to get rid of the great heat it gave off. It used so much power that each time it was switched on, the lights failed in a nearby town!

Some people called it an electronic brain. But its real name was ENIAC, short for Electronic Numerical Integrator and Calculator. ENIAC could do 5,000 calculations per second.

In the late 1940s, ENIAC's developers built a more powerful computer called EDVAC. EDVAC could work faster than ENIAC. And it could solve more complicated problems because it could "remember" instructions from its human operators. By 1959, the transistor was used in computers. This resulted in smaller computers that could do more things. But to most Americans, computers were still unusual machines that had little to do with their daily life. The time of the desktop personal computer was still years away. ∎

"Nobody thought we needed [it] . . . until we had it." This has been said about the photocopier. Could the same thing be said about any other recent invention? Write a few sentences about something that we depend on now – but did without until recently.

THEN & NOW

The early computers like ENIAC and EDVAC were marvels. In a few hours, they could solve problems that would have taken whole teams of scientists weeks or months. But these machines needed highly skilled computer experts to give them the right instructions and to run them.

Today, the personal computers in our homes and offices can store, process, and communicate more information than the most advanced computers of the 1950s. And what's more, today's computers can be operated by nearly anyone – from preschoolers to senior citizens.

Space Race

The space race began with a "beep." On October 4, 1957, the Soviet Union shocked the world by announcing that it had launched a small metal ball – about two feet in diameter – into orbit around the Earth. The satellite was called *Sputnik I*. It carried a small radio transmitter that sent a steady "beep-beep-beep" to the world as it spun around the Earth every 95 minutes.

The launch of *Sputnik* gave the Soviets a clear lead in the space race. Many Americans feared that these triumphs in space would mean Soviet victory on Earth. Senator Lyndon B. Johnson said, "With the launching of Sputniks . . . our supremacy and even our equality [have] been challenged."

To regain the lead in the space race, America needed more scientists and engineers. So Congress passed the National Defense Education Act to help schools improve math and science education. In 1958, Johnson and others created the National Aeronautics and

America Joins the Space Race

Americans reacted to the *Sputnik* launch first with shock, then with determination to win the space race. More emphasis was placed on science and math in schools. Newspapers and TV loved anything to do with outer space. This led Americans to become "space-minded." Young people idolized the American astronauts in the same way they admired sports heroes or movie stars. Adults saw the space race as part of the superpower showdown: the United States vs. the Soviet Union. Capitalism vs. communism. But as 1960 ended, no one knew who would win the race or how far into space the race would take us.

In 1957, the Soviets stunned the United States by launching Sputnik (above), the first satellite. The United States launched Echo I (below left), a communications satellite, in 1960.

Space Administration (NASA) to direct America's space efforts.

On January 31, 1958, the United States sent its first satellite, *Explorer I*, into orbit. Now the Americans and Soviets were both in space. However, many setbacks lay ahead. During 1958, half of all Soviet and American launches failed. Rockets exploded, went off course, or simply never got off the ground. One such U.S. rocket was jokingly called "Stay-putnik" or "Flopnik."

But by 1960, space launches became more successful. Soviet *Luna* probes reached the moon and photographed it. The United States launched new satellites such as *Tiros I*, the first U.S. weather satellite. It sent pictures of storms and hurricanes back from space to improve weather forecasts. And *Echo I*, a communications satellite, helped people in different countries talk to each other.

Echo I was so big and reflected so much sunlight that people easily saw it with the naked eye. It was a bright object moving swiftly across the night sky. It reminded everyone that the space age had truly begun. ■

An early UFO, or "flying saucer," photograph, taken by an amateur photographer.

UFOs: Yes or No?

In the early 1950s, *Life* magazine asked Americans, "Have We Visitors from Space?" Many people answered, "Yes!" Unidentified flying objects (UFOs) first made front-page news in the United States on June 24, 1947. Kenneth Arnold, an experienced pilot, was flying over the state of Washington. He saw nine disk-shaped objects in the sky. Arnold said the objects moved "like a saucer would if you skipped it across the water." To this day, UFOs are often called flying saucers.

Interest in UFOs continued through the 1950s. By 1955, there were more than 150 flying-saucer clubs in the United States. Many members of these clubs claimed they had met space aliens. Songs about creatures from outer space, such as "The Flying Purple People-Eater," were hits on the radio.

The U.S. Air Force took UFOs seriously. They ran a series of "projects" to analyze people's claims that they had seen UFOs. Most sightings were easy to explain. For example, people often mistake unusual-looking airplanes for UFOs. A few sightings are still labeled "unexplained." But if UFOs exist, no one has ever proved it.

Medical Successes

Many soldiers coming home from World War II owed their lives to the infection-fighting powers of penicillin, the "wonder drug." Penicillin, however, did not work against every infection.

Encouraged by penicillin's success, researchers set out to find new wonder drugs. In the late 1940s and 1950s, researchers were very successful. They found hundreds of new antibiotics — drugs that work against diseases caused by bacteria. For example, Dr. Selman A. Waksman found two new antibiotics in soil molds. One of these, streptomycin, proved to work well against tuberculosis (TB).

New Vaccines

Soon after the war ended, scientists developed a vaccine to prevent influenza (flu). The world was relieved: never again would there be a great influenza outbreak like the one that killed more than 15 million people after World War I.

More good news was on the way. In 1954, Dr. Jonas Salk began injecting people with a vaccine to prevent polio. The polio virus had crippled and paralyzed millions of people over the years. Summertime — when the disease spread most rapidly — was a fearful time. The new vaccine helped people's own bodies successfully fight the polio virus. By 1960, the Salk vaccine had ended polio's reign of terror.

Shortly after Salk, another American, Dr. Albert Sabin, developed a different polio vaccine that people could drink. The Sabin vaccine helped the body fight off the polio virus longer than Salk's. But because the Salk vaccine was so popular, people in the United States did not want to take a chance testing Sabin's vaccine. So he had to test it in the Soviet Union. Sabin's vaccine, not Salk's, stopped polio in the Soviet Union. Eventually, Sabin's vaccine became widely used in the United States too. ■

Prepare an "oral history" of the polio summers of the 1940s and 1950s. Ask people who were alive then what it was like to live in fear of the disease. Ask them for specific details ("I never drank out of a water fountain, no matter how thirsty I was"; "I was afraid to go to the movies"). Take notes about what they say. Then write an article about life before the Salk vaccine.

Dr. Jonas Salk injecting a little girl with the polio vaccine he discovered. Salk's vaccine ended polio's reign of terror in the United States.

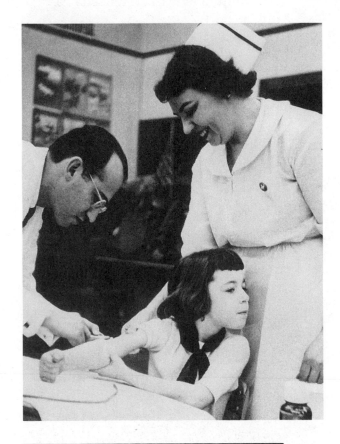

An Inventive Time

Inventors were working overtime after the war. As a result, Americans saw a steady stream of new inventions in the 1950s. And these inventions changed the way we live.

Laser Lights

Some called it a death ray. Others said it was "the light fantastic." Its official name is Light Amplification by Stimulated Emission of Radiation. But everyone came to know it as the laser. Lasers were invented in 1957. Gordon Gould, who named the laser, said, "I knew from the beginning it was the most important thing I would ever get involved with." Today, lasers are used everywhere: to cut steel, for delicate surgery, for precise measurements, even for fantastic laser light shows.

Edwin Land's Polaroid camera let people see finished photos within minutes.

Instant Photography

Photography was developed in the 1800s. Ever since, photographers wished they could instantly see the photograph they had just taken. They didn't want to wait hours or even days to see how the photo turned out. In 1947, Edwin H. Land's small daughter didn't want to wait either. "Why can't we see them now?" she asked. So Land set out to invent the Polaroid camera.

Land's camera let people see finished photos within minutes. It gave amateur photographers quick snapshots. Instant photography also helped scientists, doctors, professional photographers, and others who need quick pictures in their work.

Fantastic Plastic!

Many raw materials like rubber and metal were in short supply during World War II. Engineers quickly came up with human-made substitutes such as plastic and fiberglass. Soon, lighter, stronger plastics came out of the laboratories. Plastics began to appear everywhere—in packaging, toys, and radios, as well as things like boat hulls and automobile parts. As the space age dawned, plastics played even bigger roles in new airplanes and spacecraft.

Tapping the Sun

The newly-invented solar cell helped to power satellites and spacecraft. Solar cells use a special material that creates an electrical current from sunlight. Because solar cells use sunlight, they are perfect for powering electrical equipment in space: in space there are no clouds to block the sun. Someday, they may provide clean power for the Earth as well. ■

* This symbol before a page number indicates a photograph of the subject mentioned.

H

Hansberry, Lorraine, 44, 45
Hitler, Adolf, 6, 69
Hogan, Ben, 53
"Honeymooners, The," *34
House Un-American Activities
    Committee (HUAC), 71
"Howdy Doody," 36
Hungary, anti-Communist
    movement in, 9
Hydrogen bomb, *see* Nuclear
    energy

I

"I Love Lucy," *37–38
Independence, declarations of,
    14, *15, *16
Inflation, *defined*, 65
Integration, *see* Desegregation,
    public school; or *see*
    Montgomery bus boycott
Interstate highway system,
    *63
Iron curtain, *defined*, 9

J

Johnson, Lyndon B., 89
Johnson, Magic, 52
Jordan, Michael, 52

K

Kansas City (Philadelphia)
    Athletics, 49
Khrushchev, Nikita, 17, *20
King, Rev. Martin L., Jr.,
    82–*83
Korean War, 17–20

L

Labor-Management Relations
    Act of 1947, *see* Taft-Hartley
    Act, The
Labor unions, *64–*66
Land, Edwin H., 92
Laser, 92
Levitt, William J., 24
Levittown, New York,
    *24–*25, 61
Lilienthal, David, 84, 86
Limited war, *defined*, 18
Little Rock crisis, 78–79
Los Angeles (Brooklyn)
    Dodgers, 47, 48, 49
Luna, 90

M

MacArthur, General Douglas,
    *18–19
Mad magazine, 30
Mantle, Mickey, *48
Mao Zedong (Tse-tung), 18
Marciano, Rocky, 55
Marshall, General George C.,
    11
Marshall, Justice Thurgood,
    77, *79
Marshall Plan, The, 11–*12
Mathias, Bob, 56
Mays, Willie, 48
McCarran Internal Security
    Act of 1950, 73
McCarthy, Joseph R., *71–*74
McCarthyism, *defined*, 73
McCollum, Vashti, *76
Meany, George, 58, *66
"Mickey Mouse Club, The," 36,
    *37
Mikan, George, *51
Milwaukee (Boston) Braves,
    49
Minneapolis Lakers, 51, 52
Monnet, Jean, 67
Montgomery bus boycott,
    81–*82
Murrow, Edward R., 35, *73

N

National Aeronautics and
    Space Administration
    (NASA), 89–90
National Association for the
    Advancement of Colored
    People (NAACP), 46, 77, 79
National Basketball
    Association (NBA), 51–52
National Defense Education
    Act, 89
Nazi war crimes, *see*
    Nuremberg trials
New York Mets, 48
New York Yankees, 48
Nuclear energy: nuclear
    bombs, *84–86; nuclear
    power, 86; anti-nuclear
    groups, 86
Nuremberg trials, *68–70

P

Palmer, Arnold, 53
Parks, Rosa, 81–*82
Penicillin, 91
"Person to Person," 35
Phillips, Sam, 40
Photocopier, 87, *88
Plastic, 22, 92
Polaroid camera, *92
Polio, 91
Potsdam Conference, 8, 9
Presley, Elvis, 30, 34, 39, *40

Credits

Photo Credits

Courtesy of the Academy of Motion Picture Arts and Sciences: 26

AP/Wide World Photos: 49

Archie Comic Publications, Inc., TM and © 1992: 28

The Bettmann Archives: 2b, 10, 11, 29, 30, 31, 42a, 54ab, 55, 56, 57, 71, 72, 73, 74, 77, 78, 79, 80, 81ab, 82, 83, 85, 88b, 89b

Courtesy the Boeing Company Archives: 61ab

Courtesy C. G. Jung Institute: 45a

Courtesy Dick Clark Productions, Inc.: 39b

Courtesy the Estate of Elvis Presley: 40

Fund for UFO Research, Inc.: 90

GE Hall of History: 87a

The George Meany Memorial Archives: 66

Larry Glickman: 44

Levittown Public Library: 24, 25

Courtesy Los Angeles Dodgers, Inc.: 47

MacArthur Memorial: 18

Magnum Photos, Inc., © Elliott Erwitt: 27a

Courtesy the Maytag Company: 27b

McCollum Archive: 76

Courtesy Miles, Inc.: 35

Museum of Modern Art/Film Stills Archive: 41, 42bc

Courtesy Naismith Memorial Basketball Hall of Fame: 51, 52

Courtesy NASA: 89a

National Archives: 3b, 84

Courtesy National Automotive History Collection of the Detroit Public Library: 62b

National Library of Medicine, Bethesda, MD: 91

Courtesy New York Yankees: 48

Photofest: 34, 37ab

Courtesy Polaroid Corporate Archives: 92

Courtesy Simon and Schuster: 45a

Courtesy Simon Wiesenthal Center Archives, Los Angeles, CA: 69

Courtesy Unisys Corporation: 88a

U.S. Army Photograph: 68

Courtesy U.S. Department of Transportation Federal Highway Administration: 63b

Wayne State University, Archives of Labor and Urban Affairs: 65

Courtesy Westinghouse Electric Corporation: 87b

Wisconsin Center for Film and Theater Research: 33, 36, 45b

Courtesy Zenith Electronics Corporation: 60

Zionist Archives and Library: 16

Text Credits

The graphic on page 12 is adapted from *A History of our Country, New Edition,* by David Saville Muzzey, Copyright, 1950, by Ginn and Company. Used by permission of Silver Burdett Ginn Inc.

Quotation on page 31 from "Howl" by Allen Ginsberg. Copyright © 1956 by Allen Ginsberg. Reprinted by permission of Harper Collins Publishers.

The Texaco jingle on page 35 courtesy Texaco, Inc.

Quotations on page 38 from *The History of Television* by Rick Marschall. Copyright © by Brompton Books Corp.

Lyrics on page 39 from "Rock and Roll Is Here to Stay" by David White. Copyright © 1957 (renewed) by Arc Music Corp., Golden Music, reprinted by permission. All rights reserved.

Sam Phillips quotation on page 40 from *The Rolling Stone Illustrated History of Rock and Roll,* edited by Jim Miller. Reprinted with permission of Random House, Inc.

Excerpt on page 45 from *A Raisin in the Sun* used with permission of the Estate of Robert Nemiroff.

Althea Gibson quotation on page 54 and prizefight quotation on page 55 reprinted by permission. Copyright © 1951/1956 by The New York Times Company.

Prizefight quotation on page 55 from *The Sweet Science* by A.J. Liebling. Copyright © Penguin USA.

Melba Pattillo Beals quotation from *Eyes on the Prize* by Juan Williams. Copyright © Penguin USA.

Quotations on page 84 from *Atomic Energy; A New Start* by David Lilienthal. Copyright © 1980 by David Lilienthal. Reprinted by permission of HarperCollins Publishers.